Fusion
of the
Five Elements

Fusion
of the
Five Elements

Meditations for Transforming
Negative Emotions

Mantak Chia

Destiny Books
Rochester, Vermont

Destiny Books
One Park Street
Rochester, Vermont 05767
www.DestinyBooks.com

Destiny Books is a division of Inner Traditions International

Originally published in Thailand in 1989 by Universal Tao Publications under
the title *Fusion of the Five Elements: Basic and Advanced Meditations for Transforming Negative Emotions*

Library of Congress Cataloging-in-Publication Data
Chia, Mantak, 1944–
  Fusion of the five elements : meditations for transforming negative emotions /
Mantak Chia.
    p. cm.
  "Originally published in Thailand in 1989 by Universal Tao Publications."
  Includes index.
  ISBN-13: 978-1-59477-103-3 (pbk.)
  ISBN-10: 1-59477-103-0 (pbk.)
  1. Taoist meditations. 2. Emotions. I. Title.
  BL1942.8.C55 2007
  299.5'14435—dc22

                                                            2007000739

Printed and bound in Canada by Webcom

10 9 8 7 6 5 4 3 2 1

Text design and layout by Priscilla Baker
This book was typeset in Janson, with Sho, Present, and Futura used as display
typefaces

Contents

Acknowledgments

I wish to thank foremost those Taoist Masters who were kind enough to share their knowledge with me, never dreaming it would be so enthusiastically received by the Western world.

I thank the many contributors essential to this book's final form: The editorial and production staff at Inner Traditions/Destiny Books for their efforts to clarify the text and produce a handsome new edition of the book, Victoria Sant'Ambrogio for her line edit of the new edition, and the artist, Juan Li, for his informative illustrations.

For their assistance in producing the original edition of this book, I thank Valerie Meszaros for her dedication and thoroughness in editing the book, as well as her skill in design and production on our new desktop publishing system. I thank Charles Soupios for his editorial assistance in the technical aspects of this practice, and Michael Winn for his general editorial contributions. I thank Ivan Salgado for designing the book's original cover. I also want to extend my thanks to our publishing consultant, Joel Friedlander. His advice in establishing our desktop publishing system and in contributing to the design of the original book was invaluable.

A special thank you goes to our Thai Production Team for their cover illustration and the original book's design and layout: Raruen Keawpadung, computer graphics; Saysunee Yongyod, photographer; Udon Jandee, illustrator; and Saniem Chaisarn, production designer.

Further, I wish to express my gratitude to all instructors and students who have offered their time and advice to enhance the communication of this practice and this system.

Without my mother and my son Max, my continued efforts in bringing you the Universal Tao System would be academic. For their gifts, I offer my eternal gratitude and love.

Putting the Fusion of the Five Elements into Practice

The practices described in this book have been used successfully for thousands of years by Taoists trained by personal instruction. Readers should not undertake the practice without receiving personal transmission and training from a certified instructor of the Universal Tao, since certain of these practices, if done improperly, may cause injury or result in health problems. This book is intended to supplement individual training by the Universal Tao and to serve as a reference guide for these practices. Anyone who undertakes these practices on the basis of this book alone does so entirely at his or her own risk.

The meditations, practices, and techniques described herein are not intended to be used as an alternative or substitute for professional medical treatment and care. If any readers are suffering from illnesses based on mental or emotional disorders, an appropriate professional health care practitioner or therapist should be consulted. Such problems should be corrected before you start training.

Neither the Universal Tao nor its staff and instructors can be responsible for the consequences of any practice or misuse of the information contained in this book. If the reader undertakes any exercise without strictly following the instructions, notes, and warnings, the responsibility must lie solely with the reader.

This book does not attempt to give any medical diagnosis, treatment, prescription, or remedial recommendation in relation to any human disease, ailment, suffering, or physical condition whatsoever.

Introduction
The Foundation for Transformation

For more than five thousand years, Taoist masters researched and developed various methods to attain such desirable achievements as long life and happiness. Some of the methods they called External Alchemy, and these included the Immortal Pill, magic potions, crystals, crystal essences, flower essences, precious stones, and so forth. The highest Taoist masters realized that external methods offered only limited help while building dependencies on materials that were difficult to come by.

In their continued search for an unlimited source of energy, they turned their attention inward to uncover the mysteries surrounding their own life forces. In this search, they discovered a universe within and found it to be identical to the outer universe. They knew that the outer universe harbored a tremendous force, and that the inner universe of a human being could benefit from that force, if the two could somehow be connected.

The Taoist masters reasoned that to become connected to the outer universe, they first needed to gain control of their own inner universe. They experienced this inner universe as a flow of energy, or chi, through their bodies. The Microcosmic Orbit, running up the spine and down the front of the body, was uncovered as the pathway through which the distilled essence of this energy flows. They perceived that the Microcosmic Orbit connects three bodies—physical, soul, and spirit—within each individual and ultimately fuses them into one immortal body. It was with this perception that the study of Internal Alchemy began.

NATURAL CONNECTIONS OF
INNER AND OUTER UNIVERSES

Turning their attention toward understanding the nature and connection between the forces of the outer universe and the forces of the human body, the Taoist masters made another discovery. Each life lived in the human form is developed, structured, and influenced by a group of stars. This group of stars, which includes the planets and cosmic particles within its configuration, controls the life force, the good and bad fortune, and the birth and death of the individual.

Each day of a person's life reflects a continuing need to absorb energy from the stars and planets and from the cosmic particles. To explore the patterns of star energy in detail, ancient Taoists developed the science of astrology to a very high level.

In addition to the energy from the stars, the Taoist masters found that humans require another source of natural energy: the energy supplied by Earth's force. It is the absorption of all natural forces that nourishes the nervous system, organs, glands, senses, soul, and spirit of a human being. To facilitate their understanding of the forces of nature, the Taoists divided them into three classifications.

The first force is called the universal force (or the Original Force), and is also known as heavenly energy. It manifests as the energy of all the stars, planets, and galaxies. This vast, all-pervading force nourishes the mind, soul, and spirit of each individual and everything else in the universe that is manifest.

The universal force is especially drawn to our planet because of the unique relationship between Earth and Moon. The combined forces of Earth and Moon create a very strong magnetic power that attracts and beams down to Earth the energies of all the stars in our galaxy.

The cosmic particle force, or human plane energy, is the second force of nature. Cosmic particles are a part of the Original Force, resulting from exploded stars that have come to the end of their life cycles and are now drifting in space as very fine particles. As the strong, magnetic power created by Earth and Moon attracts many of these particles, they then drift through Earth's atmosphere as dust, and eventually become soil.

The Taoists' believe that human flesh is formed from the fallen cosmic dust of the universe. These particles, or dust, nourish the essences of the organs, glands, and senses of all humans. Humans are the highest manifestation of cosmic particle force. They can consciously gather a pure form of this energy into their bodies through meditation and ultimately return it to its primordial source.

As the third force of nature, the earth force includes the energy of plants, animals, water, and all the natural occurrences of the planet Earth. The Taoists observed that plants and trees, in their upward growth, are ever extending themselves to absorb the energy necessary to process their food. Stretching themselves to the sun and stars, and to the cosmic particles above, the plants and trees use the universal force for sustenance and growth. The animals, in turn, consume the vegetation, profiting from the cosmic energy as they do so.

Together these three forces represent the energies of heaven, humans, and earth working in harmony to sustain all existence. The ancient Taoists called the rulers of these forces the Three Pure Ones, for theirs were the first energies to emerge from the Wu Chi, the Great Emptiness (see fig. I.1 on page 4).

Traditionally, the Three Pure Ones were visualized as three emperors residing in the three palaces or centers of the body called the upper, middle, and lower tan tiens. They govern the development of the three bodies—physical, soul (or energy), and spirit—within an individual by cultivating three forces manifest in the human body as ching, chi, and shen, respectively.

VEGETABLES, ANIMALS, AND MINERALS: SOURCES OF UNIVERSAL FORCE

Humans originally were created with body cells capable of consuming and absorbing 90 percent of the cosmic forces and light to which

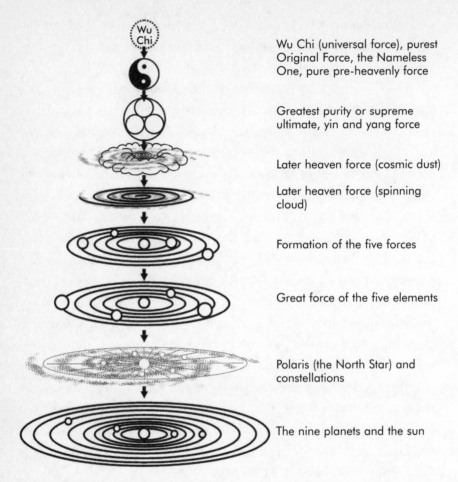

Wu Chi (universal force), purest Original Force, the Nameless One, pure pre-heavenly force

Greatest purity or supreme ultimate, yin and yang force

Later heaven force (cosmic dust)

Later heaven force (spinning cloud)

Formation of the five forces

Great force of the five elements

Polaris (the North Star) and constellations

The nine planets and the sun

Fig. I.1. Formation and continuing evolution of the universe

they were exposed. However, when we began to expend and lose our sexual energies, our cells began to deteriorate, until we were left with only a 5 to 10 percent capability of consumption and absorption. All plants, trees, and vegetation retain their ability to consume and absorb the cosmic forces and light to an 80 percent capacity, with water and nutrients supplying the remaining 20 percent of their food.

Without any consciousness about these forces, and without any practice, humans automatically continue to receive a small amount of life-force energies naturally. This is particularly true of the earth force that provides yin and yang energy (negatively and positively charged universal energy) to all the organs, glands, and senses, and provides nourishment and enhancement to the sexual organs and sexual energy of humans.

Since our body cells no longer enable us to more fully receive life force from the universal, cosmic particle, and earth forces, we must depend heavily on the vegetation, animals, and minerals comprising the earth force to do so. Since they predigest the universal force, efficiently absorbing it directly themselves, humans can depend on them to supply necessary life-force energy. Humans consume the vegetation, animals, and minerals and absorb the three main forces slowly through them. The consumption and absorption correlates with the movement of the Earth in its 365-day orbit around the sun, with the seasons of the year greatly affecting the foods consumed and the energy absorbed.

Through the practice of Fusion of the Five Elements, humans can learn about the original source of all power. They can increase their ability to absorb and transform this force directly and easily, relieving their dependence on plants and animals to convert the force for them.

THE FIVE ELEMENTS: THE ORIGINAL FORCES

The Taoists further classified all things in the universe making up the universal force, the cosmic particle force, and the earth force as correspondences of the "five elements," "five phases," or "five interacting" forces of nature. That is, each force originates from and is controlled by the five elements of nature. These are earth, metal, fire, wood, and water.

The Origins of the Five Elements of Nature

Taoists believe that the five elements of nature originated as five huge stars, given birth by the Three Pure Ones out of the Wu Chi. These five stars (or five elements), in turn, gave birth to the entire universe, including trillions of stars. They created the North Star, which created smaller stars, including five major constellations. From the constellations, the planets arose, including the planet Earth. The five constellations have a direct relationship with five planets, five seasons on Earth, five directions of Earth, and five major organs of the human body (fig. I.2).

The Taoists consider the forces of the five elements to be "grand forces," and sometimes refer to them in this way.

1. The grand force of water created the Northern Constellation and the planet Mercury. It manifests as the northern direction of the earth force and the winter season. It corresponds to the human water force of the kidneys and bladder. Its energy has an inwardly gathering quality.

2. The grand force of fire created the Southern Constellation

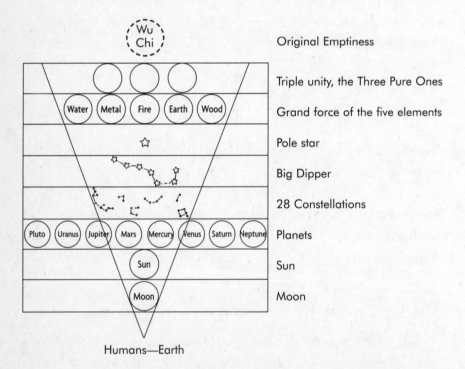

Fig. I.2. The universe

and the planet Mars. It manifests as the southern direction of the earth force and the summer season. It corresponds to the human fire force of the heart and small intestine. Its energy has an expanding, developing quality.

3. The grand force of wood created the Eastern Constellation and the planet Jupiter. It manifests as the eastern direction of the earth force and the spring season. It corresponds to the human wood force of the liver and gall bladder. Its energy has a generating quality.

4. The grand force of metal created the Western Constellation and the planet Venus. It manifests as the western direction of the earth force and the fall season. It corresponds to the human metal force of the lungs and large intestine. Its energy has a contracting quality.

5. The grand force of earth created the Central Constellation and the planet Saturn. It manifests as the central direction of the earth force and the Indian summer season. It corresponds to the human earth force of the spleen, stomach, and pancreas. Its energy has a stabilizing quality.

To make connections between and to gain control of the inner and outer universes, the Taoists developed the Fusion of the Five Elements practice. Fusion begins with understanding the dynamics of the universe, the planet Earth, and the human body with respect to their relationships to the five elements of nature.

FUSION OF THE FIVE ELEMENTS PRACTICE

Fusion of the Five Elements, marking the beginning of the Taoist practice of Internal Alchemy, focuses on the interaction and fusion of all five elements and their correspondences, and their transformation into a harmonious whole of high-quality energy. During this process, the essence of life-force energy found in the organs, glands, and senses is transformed, purified, condensed, and combined with the universal force. The new form of energy that emerges through this process can effect positive changes in the human body.

To effect positive changes in the human body, the Taoists first focus on the negative aspects or weaknesses to transform them into strengths. They uncover weaknesses by focusing on what is known as the counteracting or controlling forces of the five elements. This means studying the effects of the five elements upon each other.

In studying the energy of the liver, for example, the organ associated with the planet Jupiter and the wood element, Taoists discovered that its energy can be counteracted or controlled by the energy of the lungs, associated with the planet Venus and the metal element. That is, the metal element controls the wood element, and the lungs control the liver. Similarly, the energy of the kidneys, associated with the planet Mercury and the water element, can be counteracted by the energy of the heart, associated with the planet Mars and the element fire. This means the water element controls the fire element, and the kidneys control the heart. All five elements have a counteracting force (fig. I.3).

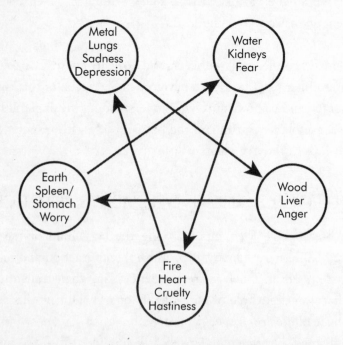

Fig. I.3. Counteracting cycle

The interaction of the two elements of water and fire is an easy one to comprehend. The heat of fire can evaporate water, thereby controlling it. If this is true, then the reverse is also true: fire can be counteracted or controlled by the water element. Water can extinguish fire. The Taoists considered the interactions of the five elements as two distinct cycles existing in nature—the creative cycle and the counteracting or controlling cycle. Both are equally important in sustaining life, but need to be balanced and in control if things are to be kept running smoothly. Both cycles help determine which of your organs are weak and which are strong. You will study them in depth in the Fusion practice, beginning with the counteracting or controlling cycle and your negative emotions in Fusion I.

To utilize the two cycles effectively, it is important to determine your strengths and weaknesses. The planetary associations can play a major role in your conceptualization, because there are months or years in which certain stars and/or planets can come very close to Earth and can greatly influence your behavior.

For example, if you have a weak liver, when the planet Venus (the metal star associated with the lungs) comes close to Earth, your liver energy can be depleted. This can cause emotional outbursts of anger and indecisiveness, the negative emotions of the liver. If you do not know that you need to strengthen the liver energy at these times, and how to find a balance to your energy, you will be affected by such planetary events. This will affect all phases of your life. Eventually you will be overcome. When the liver is overly depleted by the intervention of the stars, the planets, the earth force, and other forces, recharging itself with energy will become very difficult. This is because it is in a weakened state. Then, when a charge of energy does come, the liver will not be able to fully utilize it. If the cycle continues and the counteracting forces of the stars, planets, Earth, and other sources approach again, the liver will be further depleted, now retaining little or no energy. This can cause tremendous suffering in all aspects of your life.

Using all the chapters of Fusion I presented in this book will help you to create balance before delving into what star or planet influences you. The Fusion I practices provides a degree of creative and counteracting balances automatically. You will discover how wood and metal (liver and lungs) counteract each other, and will feel how they can be balanced automatically by the earth force. The weaker one will be strengthened. The overly strong one will be toned down by its opposing force. With neither one too weak nor too strong, they will become harmonious allies and not enemies of each other. In the Fusion II practices, which are presented in the next book in this series, you will delve deeper, as you conscientiously search for your influencing stars and planets and use the cycles to promote greater strengths for your weaknesses.

During the Fusion practice, the negative emotions associated with each organ, and so, each element, are drawn out of the organs and transformed into a neutralized energy, thereby "balancing the weather" of the body's total energies. This neutralized energy can be blended with positive energies, also residing in the organs, and transformed into pure life-force energy. The Taoists have a saying: "Refined red sand turns into silver." This means that if you fuse all the different kinds of emotional energy together, they will adhere into a harmonious whole. However, unrefined, "unfused" energy will have the quality of sand, scattered about and unable to stick together.

THE PEARL: ESSENCE OF HUMAN BODY AND ENERGY BODY

The pure life-force energy derived from the organs and fused together during the Fusion practice is crystallized into an energy ball. This energy ball can be perceived as a crystal or diamond, but is perceived most commonly as a radiant pearl. Forming the pearl is the first step toward transferring consciousness to a new realm.

Not all people perceive the pearl in the same way. Some might not see a pearl, but might recognize it as an acute feeling of awareness or as an intensified ability to concentrate. Some may feel a concentration of heat. All are experiencing the pearl as the essence of life-force energy.

This pearl is then circulated in the Microcosmic Orbit. While circulating, the pearl activates and absorbs the universal and earth forces. It also uses them to strengthen and purify the physical body, particularly the organs, glands, and senses. Later, the pearl plays a central role in developing and nourishing the soul body or energy body. It is developed further in the higher-level Kan and Li meditations.

Balanced energy not only is very desirable for the health of the organs, glands, and senses, but also is basic to the formation of a pearl. Thus, balanced energy is a very important element of Fusion. Also of great importance to the Fusion practice is the function of the pearl in opening, cleansing, purifying, and protecting specific channels that run through the body. These channels are the Thrusting Channels (cleansing and protecting channels), the Belt Channel (a protecting channel), and the Great Regulator and Great Bridge Channels (channels binding together and regulating, respectively, energy flow through all the body's acupuncture meridians).

All levels of Fusion practice clean and purify the organs and the body.

Fusion of the Five Elements I

The Fusion I practices make use of *pakuas* and energy collection points to balance, connect, and draw out negative emotional energies found in the organs. These energies, along with their corresponding glands' and senses' energies, are then fused and transformed into pure life-force energy.

The purity of this energy has an adhering and magnetizing quality, which enables it to condense into a pearl of refined energy. The practitioner then uses the pearl to form the soul or energy body that will connect to the universal, cosmic particle, and earth forces, whose energies become part of the pearl.

Collecting the organs' energies in no way diminishes their

strength. In fact, each time you practice Fusion, the essence energies collected from the organs are fused, purified, and transformed into an improved quality of life-force energy. Each time you finish the practice, the improved quality energy in the form of the pearl disperses. This energy returns to enhance all of the organs and glands, particularly those that require additional energy. The dispersed energy also provides protection to the physical and soul body.

Fusion of the Five Elements II

Fusion II focuses on using the pearl to grow or intensify the energy of good virtue. It uses the creative cycle to circulate the positive chi of virtuous energy through the major organs. All the energy gathered during this cycle combines to form a pearl of compassion energy. Practitioners then use this pearl to open and cleanse the Thrusting Channels, and to open the protective Belt Channel that surrounds the Thrusting Channels.

Fusion of the Five Elements III

Fusion III opens the Great Regulator and Great Bridge Channels, combines all (eight) special channels together and sets them all into motion. Practitioners develop more physical protection through this process.

The entire Fusion practice is a step-by-step procedure of purifying yourself and controlling your own inner force. By creating the pure energy pearl and fusing the forces of the five elements to create a new, better, and purer life force, you will gain the power of self-mastery. You can use this energy externally, to call forth directly the universal and earth forces to empower and protect you. In this way the organs, glands, and senses comprising and supplying the life force to the human body finally are reconnected to the stars, the planets, and the cosmic particles from which they emerged.

DESCRIPTION OF FUSION I

Basic Practice

The Fusion practice is a meditation consisting of nine chapters. In the basic Fusion practice, described in chapters 1 through 5, the student works with the five elemental forces of humans. In the advanced practice, described in chapters 6 through 9, the student continues on to work with the five elemental forces of the earth and also with the five elemental forces of the universe. Although you can practice Fusion I by successfully completing the basic practice, you will attain the full benefit by continuing through the advanced procedures.

Chapter 1: Forming the Four Pakuas, Blending Energy, and Forming the Pearl at the Center of Control

The word *pa* means "eight"; *kua* means "symbol." The pakua is an eight-sided, three-dimensional crystal that draws energies from the organs, glands, and senses to be refined, transformed, condensed, and stored.

1. You begin this process by building four pakuas to refine, condense, and store the energy.
2. At the center of the body between the four pakuas, you create a "self-center"—a center of being or center of control called the cauldron.
3. As the four pakuas draw the energy into the cauldron at your center of being, the energy is fused or crystallized into a life-force energy sphere or ball, a pearl of condensed energy. (The pearl is sometimes referred to as the inner pill or human pill.) This pearl then is circulated in the Microcosmic Orbit.

Chapter 2: Balancing the Organ Energy to Experience Inner Peace and Harmony

1. To balance the organ energy, you first form the collection points for the organs.

2. Then you draw, collect, and blend the different qualities (kidneys [cold/wet], heart [hot], liver [warm, moist], lungs [cool, dry], and spleen [mild]) into the collection points. This energy is moved to the front pakua, which is considered the controlling pakua.

3. You form the back pakua and blend and refine the residual energies of the organs in the back collection points.

4. You spiral, draw, and condense all the energies from the front and back pakuas into the cauldron.

5. Similarly, you form the right and left side pakuas to collect any remaining organ energy. You blend and refine the energy in these pakuas, and then bring their combined energies into the cauldron.

6. In the cauldron all the energies are condensed into a pearl again. Then the pearl is moved to the Microcosmic Orbit for circulation.

Chapter 3: Connecting the Senses with the Organs, Controlling the Senses, Sealing the Openings, Overcoming Temptations

1. To strengthen and control the senses and prevent the sense energy from scattering, you will learn that the relationship between each pair of organs and senses is like the relationship of parents and children.

2. You will turn the senses inward and draw them into the organs and their collection points. As in chapter 2, you move the energy into all four pakuas. In the pakuas, the energy is refined, and then it is condensed into the cauldron, the center of control, where the pearl is formed. The pearl now consists of the crystallized essences of the senses and organs, and again can be moved to and circulated in the Microcosmic Orbit.

Chapter 4: Transforming the Negative Emotions of Each Organ into Useful Energy

1. During thousands of years of exploring philosophy and psychology, the Taoists realized the need to explore basic human emo-

tions. They observed that certain emotions, if not understood and dealt with, will attract or create other undesirable emotions. The Taoists believe that all emotions originate from the organs, and that the mind regulates and determines their use. Although the emotional energies that can be sensed within an organ are not limited, certain specific, basic negative emotions are associated with each organ, and these are addressed in chapter 4:

- Kidneys—fear
- Heart—impatience, hastiness
- Liver—anger
- Lungs—sadness, depression
- Spleen—worry

2. As in chapters 2 and 3, you blend and transform these energies in the front pakua, and create the back, left, and right side pakuas. In these four pakuas you will refine the energy, condense it into the cauldron to form a pearl, and circulate the pearl in the Microcosmic Orbit.

Chapter 5: Creating the Pearl that Forms the Energy Body

1. In chapter 5, you will combine the practices of all the previous chapters. First you put the senses in contact with the organs and collect the organ and emotional energy in the collection points. You bring this energy to all four pakuas and blend the energies there. This energy then refines and condenses into the cauldron to form a pearl.

2. The pearl you create is projected from the physical body and controlled in the space above you. In its out-of-body condition, the pearl is formed into the energy body.

3. You form the energy body into an image that you would like your physical body to be. You can give it a name at this time to make it easier to summon as you continue your practice.

4. You transfer the Microcosmic Orbit to the energy body from the physical body as the first experience of a transference of consciousness.

5. A protective shield is formed around the energy body, and a great bubble is formed encasing both the energy and physical bodies. At the end of this chapter, the protective shield is reabsorbed while the great bubble shrinks down over the physical body to protect it. You can build upon this layer with subsequent layers of protection as your practice continues.

Advanced Practice

The advanced practice of Fusion I incorporates the five chapters learned in the basic practice, and so it involves working with the five elemental forces of humans. However, after completing chapter 4, and before proceeding with forming the energy body in chapter 5, it is best to first practice chapters 6 and 7 of the advanced practice to create a more powerful pearl to work with. Then, using the greatly refined and radiant energy of this pearl, you can create an energy body that now benefits from three additional sources of energy: the earth, cosmic particle, and universal forces. Then you proceed with this energy body to experience the remaining formulas.

The advanced practice formulas make use of images that enhance the organs' energies as you continue to refine the pearl.

Chapter 6: Forming the Virgin Children and Their Animal Offspring to Connect to the Universal, Cosmic Particle, and Earth Forces

When the organ energy is very pure, you can project it and crystallize it into the image of a virgin boy or girl as the purest form of the virtue energy of the organs. Each virgin child's breath, in turn, creates an animal as its offspring. The children and animals can be used as protection for the physical body by connecting them to form protective rings. The pearl is the center of the gathering of the children and animals. You can substitute other images from your personal mythology, such as a ring of saints, warrior-heroes, jewels, or other significant images. If you circulate a pearl in the Microcosmic Orbit while under the protection of the children and animals' rings, and connect the pearl to the universal, cosmic particle, and earth forces, you can bring those energies to the children and animals. They, in turn, can deliver this energy to the organs, glands, and senses for increased life force.

Chapter 7: Calling Forth the Earth Force to Empower and Protect

When you have established a very pure organ energy, you can project it out of the body to call forth or attract the earth force to you. Once you have attracted this force, you form the animal images, or other earth images such as flowers or trees, that will help you retain it. Then you use the animals to form a ring of fire to empower the organs and protect them. At this point, refer again to chapter 5 and create a more powerful energy body.

Chapter 8: Calling Forth the Planets' and Stars' Forces to Empower and Protect

In this formula you will form pearls of pure organ energy to attract the planet that corresponds to each organ. The purpose is to draw on the forces of the planets and add them to the forces of the virgin children, the internal animals, and the animals formed from the earth elemental forces for empowerment and protection.

Chapter 9: Transferring Consciousness to the Energy Body in this Life Brings Immortality

The energy body serves as vehicle for consciousness, tapping on a higher source of energy and bringing this higher energy back into the physical body. In the physical body it can be transformed into a more usable energy.

1. Transferring the life-force energy, or chi, to the energy body will enable you to use the energy body to support the spirit body.
   - The physical body is like a boat and its engine.

- The energy (chi) body is the fuel, or steam, providing force.
- The spirit body is the captain, who commands.

2. The functions of the energy body are to transfer the essence of life (energies of organs, glands, and senses) consciously into the spirit body and to push the spirit body into the Mid-Plane.

Formula 1

Forming the Four Pakuas, Blending Energy, and Forming the Pearl at the Center of Control

Chapters 1 through 5 describe how to transform emotional energy into a useful energy, and in the process, how to achieve a balanced state of inner peace and harmony. Your goal in practicing the basic steps of the Fusion I meditation is to develop your awareness of the pearl of energy that you create.

THEORY: FOUR PAKUAS AND THE CAULDRON

The eight sides that form a pakua represent the eight natural forces of the universe. These are the forces of 1) wind, 2) thunder, 3) mountains, 4) water, 5) the heavens, 6) metal, 7) earth, 8) fire (see fig. 1.1 on page 20).

Construction of the Pakua

We can perceive a pakua as an octagon formed from eight trigrams. However, to simplify the creation of a pakua for meditation, we can envision an image formed of a simple web pattern. This image consists

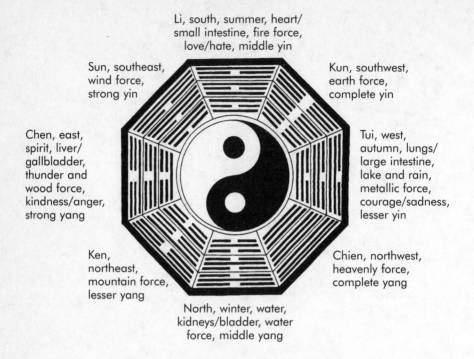

Li, south, summer, heart/
small intestine, fire force,
love/hate, middle yin

Sun, southeast,
wind force,
strong yin

Kun, southwest,
earth force,
complete yin

Chen, east,
spirit, liver/
gallbladder,
thunder and
wood force,
kindness/anger,
strong yang

Tui, west,
autumn, lungs/
large intestine,
lake and rain,
metallic force,
courage/sadness,
lesser yin

Ken,
northeast,
mountain force,
lesser yang

Chien, northwest,
heavenly force,
complete yang

North, winter, water,
kidneys/bladder, water
force, middle yang

Fig.1.1. The eight sides of the pakua
represent the eight natural forces of the universe.

of three eight-sided layers—similar to the eight-sided, multilayered cut of a diamond—with spokes connecting each layer. The outer, largest layer of the pakua is three inches (7.62 centimeters) in diameter. At the center is a Tai Chi (yin/yang) symbol that spirals to blend and transform the force. At the back of the pakua, the diamondlike shape of the image is realized further as all eight sides of the pakua create a funnel shape that converges at one central point.

We trace the pakua with the mind in meditation, drawing it in layers, beginning with the outer, three-inch octagon, then continuing inward with the second and third levels. All are drawn in either a clockwise or counterclockwise direction. Then we create the eight spokes to connect the layers. These spokes come together at the Tai Chi symbol placed at the center of the pakua. After we have the shape well memorized, we can recreate it simply by visualization (fig. 1.2).

Fig. 1.2. Simple pakua for beginning the practice

Location of the Four Pakuas

The four pakuas are located as follows:

1. Front (or navel) pakua: Behind the navel, about one and a half inches inside.*
2. Back pakua: At the Door of Life, at the back of the body directly opposite the navel between Lumbar 2 and 3, and about one and a half inches in.
3. Left pakua: On the left side of the body, at the intersection of a mentally drawn line extending vertically downward from the left armpit, and a line extending horizontally to the left side from the level of the navel and the Door of Life. The pakua is about one and a half inches (3.8 centimeters) in from this intersection point.

---

*The measurements pertain to an average-sized body, but can vary for a smaller or larger person.

4. Right pakua: On the right side of the body, at the intersection of a visualized vertical line drawn down from the right armpit, and a horizontal line drawn from the level of the navel and the Door of Life, to about one and a half inches in.

Energy is brought into these pakuas, where it is then blended and transformed.

Location of the Cauldron: The Point of Control

The cauldron is considered the center of the body. It is located in the space between the navel and the Door of Life, but more toward the back of the body, in front of the kidneys. It is three inches in diameter. It is the place where prenatal force, as part of the universal or original force, was formed. It is also the place where all of the five elemental forces combine and transform into a very refined energy.

1. The energy from each of the four pakuas is balanced and condensed at their Tai Chi centers, and these centers can glow with white or golden light.
2. The Tai Chi centers of the four pakuas spiral and blend this energy and direct it through the funnel-like backs of the pakuas into the cauldron. The center of the cauldron is usually at a point level with the Door of Life, although the center can vary with each person as much as an inch and a half up or down. In men who are top-heavy, the center can be lower. Women who are bottom-heavy can have a higher center. It seems that the thinner the person, the greater the chance the center point will be at the same level as the Door of Life and the navel. Once you have found it, you will readily know it is your center of awareness.
3. The front and back pakuas function as a pair in spiraling, drawing, refining, and condensing the energy into the cauldron.
4. The two side pakuas constitute a second pair to spiral, draw, refine, and condense the energy into the cauldron.

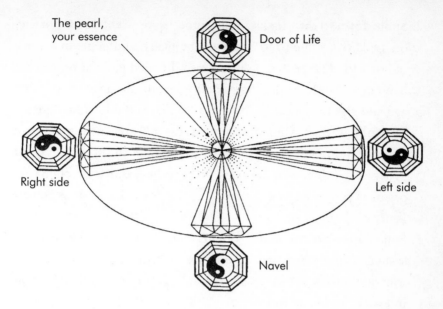

The pearl,
your essence

Door of Life

Right side

Left side

Navel

Fig. 1.3. Four pakuas and condensing energy into a pearl

5. At the cauldron, energies are mixed further, blended, and condensed, and the pearl is formed (fig. 1.3).

 Practice of Formula 1

Sit up properly. Feel the feet touching the ground, the hands holding together, and the tongue touching the palate.

Practice the Inner Smile

1. Practice the Inner Smile meditation to relax the mind and the body. Feel the smiling energy, like sunshine, collect in the eyes and the third eye. Let all the facial muscles relax. Feel the outer corners of your eyelids and mouth uplift. Smile down, and feel the smiling energy slowly flow down to the neck, thymus gland, and heart. Feel the heart open. Create a state of love, joy, and happiness in the heart.

2. Smile down to the organs and become aware of the virtues of each organ as you smile to it: Smile to the heart, and generate a sense of honor and respect, as you increase the feelings of love, joy, and happiness. Smile to the lungs, and generate the feelings of courage and righteousness in the lungs. Smile to the liver, and generate kindness in it. Smile to the pancreas and spleen, and generate fairness and openness in those organs. Smile to the kidneys, and generate gentleness in the kidneys. Feel the positive effect on each organ as you smile to it. Be aware of the positive emotions you are generating (fig. 1.4).

3. Smile down to the sexual organs. Smile down to the digestive system. Generate a creative energy. Feel the energy flow all the way down with the saliva as you swallow to your stomach, small intestine, and large intestine.

4. Return to the eyes. Smile in to your pituitary and pineal glands. Smile into the left and right hemispheres to balance the brain, and then smile all the way down the spinal cord.

5. Return to the eyes again, and smile down the front, middle, and back line. Well-trained students can practice the Inner Smile at a fast pace.

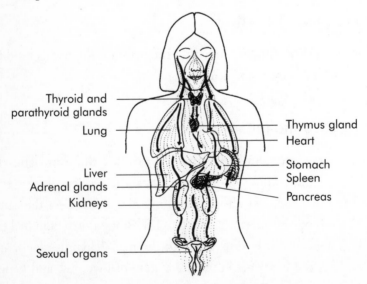

Fig. 1.4. Smile down to the organs.

❂ Form the Front Pakua

1. Turn your awareness and senses inward toward the navel. Concentrate on the navel, and bring all the energies you have generated there. Feel their warmth. As you smile to the navel, blend and condense these energies into a ball of energy inside the navel area.
2. Look inward. Turn all the senses inward in preparation for constructing the pakua.
3. Beginning at a point one and a half inches (3.8 centimeters) inside and a little above the navel, draw with the mind the first line of the pakua. (Those who have visualization or kinesthetic problems can trace the lines of the pakua with a finger.)
4. Continue constructing all eight lines of the outer layer of the pakua.
5. Begin the second layer, constructing it one line at a time.
6. Begin the third layer, drawing eight lines again.
7. Now, one at a time, draw the eight spokes from the outer layer through the inner layer. Picture the Tai Chi symbol in the middle, and as you draw each spoke, continue it into the Tai Chi.
8. Lastly, let the Tai Chi symbol spiral in either direction (but preferably clockwise) as it gradually blends and transforms the energy. Now the pakua can glow with white light. Some people will sense a stronger ability to concentrate at this time.
9. Rest and experience this glowing light and warmth.

❂ Form the Back Pakua

1. Beginning at a point about one and a half inches in and a little above the Door of Life, mentally trace the first, outer layer.
2. Construct the second layer.
3. Construct the third layer.
4. Draw the eight spokes through the three layers toward the Tai Chi visualized at the center of the pakua.
5. Spiral the Tai Chi at the center, and sense the center glowing with white light.
6. Rest and experience the glowing light.

Notice that the back pakua is identical to the front pakua. Future references to forming the back pakua mention a simpler procedure of copying the front pakua to the back.

☯ Spiral the Front and Back Pakua Energy to the Cauldron

1. Divide your concentration between the front and back pakuas.
2. Spiral the two pakuas, especially their Tai Chi centers. Initially you can spiral without worrying about moving in a particular direction. Eventually, you can use your mind to train the spirals of each of the pakuas to spin in the direction you choose. With your inner eye, direct the energy along the road or pathway of the spiral.
3. Become aware of the funnel-like shape of the backs of the pakuas. As you spiral, feel the force being drawn in from the pakuas through their funnel-like backs toward the cauldron. Then concentrate more on the cauldron end of the spiral to help draw the energy into the cauldron. When you feel the energy at the cauldron, condense it and stop spiraling.
4. The condensed energy can glow with white light. Some people will simply feel a greater awareness of the navel area.

☯ Form the Right-Side Pakua

1. Concentrate on the point on the right side of the body, below the armpit and level with the navel, and approximately one and a half inches in. Trace the first, outer layer of this pakua.
2. Draw the eight lines of the second layer.
3. Draw the eight lines of the third layer.
4. Draw the eight spokes into a Tai Chi symbol at the middle of the pakua. Spiral the symbol, and it should glow with light.

❂ Form the Left-Side Pakua

1. Concentrate on the point on the left side of the body, below the armpit and level with the navel, and approximately one and a half inches in. Trace the first layer of this pakua.
2. Follow the directions in steps 2 through 4 for the right side.

Notice that the right and left pakuas are identical to the front and back pakuas. Future references to forming the right and left pakuas mention a simpler procedure of copying the front and back pakuas to the right and left sides.

❂ Spiral the Left and Right Pakua Energy into the Cauldron

1. Spiral the centers from the right and left side pakuas to draw the glowing energy into the cauldron at the center of the body. You can direct the spirals clockwise, counterclockwise, or simply let the spirals move in any direction. Increase the spirals at the cauldron to draw into it the energy of the left and right pakuas. At the cauldron, join this energy with the energy from the front and back pakuas. Although the cauldron may not necessarily be exactly at the center of the four points, it is considered the center of your body, or your center of being. You may see the cauldron glowing brighter as more energy condenses and fuses together, or you may feel more centered and have stronger concentration.
2. Divide your concentration among the cauldron, the front and back pakuas, and the left and right pakuas (see fig. 1.5 on page 28).
3. Continue to spiral more energy to the cauldron.

❂ Form a Pearl

1. In a mild and relaxed manner, mentally concentrate and turn all the senses downward to the cauldron while continuing to spiral.

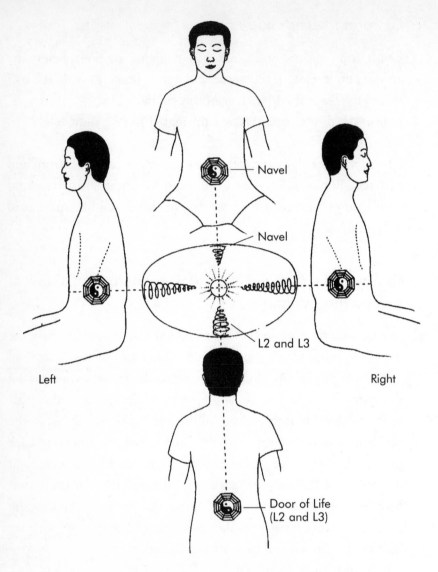

Navel

Navel

L2 and L3

Left

Right

Door of Life
(L2 and L3)

Fig. 1.5. Four pakuas: spiraling to form the pearl

You should feel no tension, but rather, keep a simple awareness of the energy that is condensing there.

2. Form the pearl that is the highly condensed essence of your life-force energy. It is the essence of your organs, glands, senses, and mind and will absorb the impure energy of the organs and glands,

purify it, and return it to them as a higher form of energy. The pearl can control the organs and glands, and it helps establish the cauldron firmly.

⊙ Anchor and Program the Pearl through Verbal Affirmations

1. When you begin to feel the energy condensing at your center, relax a bit more and turn all your senses, attention, and awareness into the pearl. As you relax sufficiently, you will feel your energy stabilizing and the pearl becoming stronger and clearer in your awareness.
2. At the peak of these sensations of centeredness and stability, anchor in and program this experience with the pearl. Associating yourself with your center anchors your center to the pearl. Use a verbal affirmation such as:

- I feel deeply centered, clear, and calm; external forces do not move me.
- I am under my own control; I feel grounded and centered.
- My energy is stable and clear; I am emotionally balanced.

⊙ Move the Pearl into the Microcosmic Orbit

As the pearl moves in the Microcosmic Orbit, you will feel three sources of energy. The universal force of the North Star (Polaris) and the Big Dipper constellation supplies energy through your crown. Cosmic particles fall to Earth, and this energy (cosmic particle force) combines with the smiling energy supplied at the mid-eyebrow. The third source of energy is the earth force, and it is supplied at the perineum through the soles of the feet. Be aware of the combined energy from these three sources as you circulate the Microcosmic Orbit (sometimes more simply referred to as the Microcosmic), running up the Governor Channel (along the spine of the body), over the crown of the head, and down the Functional Channel (along the front, center of the body).

Note: Drawing the energy into and running it through the pathway of the Microcosmic Orbit are crucial steps in Fusion of the Five Elements and all Universal Tao practices. It is also very helpful to your Fusion practice to know the Healing Love and Iron Shirt exercises. They will help you generate more energy and ease and strengthen the flow of energy.*

1. Move the pearl down to the perineum, the Gate of Life and Death, by focusing on, lightly contracting, and pulling up the perineum. Feel the downward pull on the pearl.
2. Sense the pearl as a bright star shining in the dark at the bottom of your body's trunk. The pleasant, cool, blue energy of the earth now enters through the perineum. Some will see the blue color while others will feel a gentle, soft, kind energy. This energy enhances the feeling of grounding. At this point you may anchor in feelings of security, safety, and grounding by using a verbal affirmation. For example: "I am safe, secure, and grounded in my daily life."
3. Pull up on the back part of the anus toward the sacrum and move the pearl from the perineum to the coccyx.
4. Tilt the sacrum to adjust the alignment of the coccyx with the earth force until you feel more centered and grounded. Feel the coccyx shine with light as the pearl reaches and then passes through it. Again, use a verbal affirmation of the feelings of being centered and grounded.
5. Move the pearl to the Door of Life and feel it glow, enhancing the feeling of softness and gentleness.

---

*"The Microcosmic Orbit is opened by sitting in meditation for a few minutes each morning as you practice the Inner Smile. It is much easier to cultivate your energy if you first understand the major paths of energy circulation in the body. . . . When the tongue is touched to the roof of the mouth just behind the front teeth, the energy can flow in a circle up the spine and down the front of the body. . . . Begin in the eyes and allow your mind to circulate with the energy as it travels down the front of your body through your tongue, throat, chest, and navel and then up the tailbone and spine to the head. Feel the energy circulate through the Microcosmic Orbit by letting your mind flow along with it." From Mantak Chia, *Iron Shirt Chi Kung* (Rochester, Vt.: Destiny Books, 2006), 60.

6. Now move the pearl up to T11 and feel it radiate with light.

7. Move the pearl to C7. Let C7 glow and burn off any burdens that you may feel. Now use an affirmation to program your feelings of lightness and well-being.

8. Move the pearl to the base of the skull (Jade Pillow). Let this point glow with bright light.

9. Move the pearl to the crown, and fill the crown with light. Feel the warmth of the universal force of the North Star and the Big Dipper as that energy now enters through the crown. If you have the capacity to see colors, the color of the North Star is purple, while the Big Dipper has a red light in its center. Feel the loving, strong force.

10. Continue to be aware of the pathway of the Microcosmic Orbit as you move the pearl down to the third eye point at mid-eyebrow. Feel the gentle, smiling energy combine with the cosmic particle force as it is drawn in through the mid-eyebrow. If you can visualize color, see this force as golden. Feel its firm, strong, determined force.

11. Feel the mid-eyebrow point glow with light, and feel a sense of purpose. Use another verbal affirmation to program the pearl with your sense of purpose and vision.

12. Move the pearl down to the throat, and burn off any negative energy you may find.

13. Move the pearl to the heart and feel love, joy, and happiness. The heart is an excellent point to use a verbal affirmation expressing greater love and joy in your life.

14. Move the pearl to the solar plexus point, and then down to the navel.

15. Beginners may lose the pearl by losing their concentration. If your pearl is lost or diminished at any time during the Fusion practice, start over and form a new pearl. Once again become aware of the four pakuas, and condense the energy into a pearl. At first, forming a new pearl will take time, but as your practice continues, you will build up larger amounts of residual energy. The more energy

you have readily available, the easier and faster it is to form a pearl. Bring the new pearl to the perineum, and circle it in the Microcosmic Orbit. Be very aware of the pearl as it moves.

16. Turn a portion of your consciousness to the four pakuas as the pearl moves through the Orbit. Feel the energy flow through the spirals to the cauldron at the center of the four pakuas and continually enhance the pearl.

17. Now circulate the pearl in the Microcosmic Orbit a little faster. Be aware of the pathway the pearl follows (fig. 1.6).

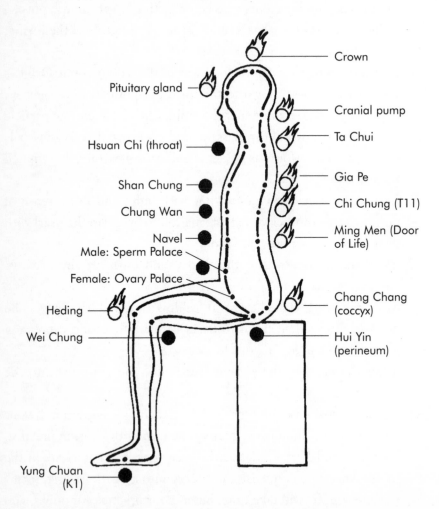

Fig. 1.6. Pathway of the Microcosmic Orbit

18. Be aware of the universal force, the North Star with purple light and the Big Dipper with red light, both above your head, the cosmic particle force in front of you, and the earth force under your feet. Feel these energies as they are supplied to you (fig. 1.7).

19. This is the time to balance the energy that you feel flowing through the Microcosmic Orbit. If you feel the flowing energy is too warm, draw in more earth energy through the perineum. If you feel that the energy is too cool, draw in more universal energy through the

Fig. 1.7. Microcosmic Orbit—universal, earth, and human forces

crown. If you feel you are losing concentration, draw in more of the fallen cosmic particle energy through the mid-eyebrow.

⟳ Collect the Energy

Bring the energy to the navel, hold the energy here for a while, and then bring the energy behind the navel to the cauldron. Feel its warmth, and then collect the energy at the cauldron.

⟳ Finish with Chi Massage

End the exercise with Chi Massage. Rub your hands together, and then use the warmed hands to rub the face, throat, and so on. (You can review Chi Massage in Mantak Chia, *Chi Self-Massage: The Taoist Way of Rejuvenation* [Rochester, Vt.: Destiny Books, 2006].)

CENTERING AWARENESS IN THE PEARL

The immediate, practical use of the pearl in daily life is to help center your awareness so that your environment does not throw you out of balance. The deeper purpose of mastering the first formula is to lay an unshakable foundation for achieving oneness with the universal force.

To center awareness in the pearl is to find the center, or control point, of your soul. The shining pearl, as the essence of your soul, is always in touch with the source of universal force within yourself. Centering your awareness in the pearl places you in the position of mastery of your inner spiritual life as well as mastery of the outer earth and cosmic particle forces that contribute to your daily life.

As you more frequently practice the Fusion meditation and strengthen your ability to center your awareness in your pearl, you will discover that you can tune in to your higher energies during your spare moments each day. You will find your intuitive mind growing sharper and clearer, more creative ideas will pop up in your work, and your capacity to love your family and friends will increase dramatically.

Negative patterns in your life that mindlessly disperse your life energy, such as daydreaming, the distraction of television, or negative emotional ruminations, can be defeated. The deep feelings of longing, loss, jealousy, or hostility that emerge from the negative patterns can be overcome.

As you use your idle moments throughout the day to engage in the Fusion practice, your awareness maintains the presence of your pearl. Your soul essence is busy giving birth to creative thoughts, realistic goals, and spontaneous feelings appropriate to the immediate moment. At the same time, negative input from your vital organs or from your environment dissolves in the center cauldron and is greeted with fresh, strong energy from the universe. Your life will begin to overflow with radiance and a surplus of energy that can become joy, kindness, creativity, and love.

It is wise to keep a steady contact with the universal force by regularly calling upon your pearl/soul essence. If you remain continuously aware of the pearl in your daily life, your connection to the Tao will become more powerful, making your life happy, harmonious, and effortless.

Formula 2

Balancing the Organ Energy to Experience Jnner Peace and Harmony

Each organ (and its secondary organ, set in parentheses in this section) has a collection point for its particular quality of energy. Keep in mind the organs' correspondences to the five elements and to the seasons of the universal and earth forces. (See "The Five Elements: The Original Forces" in the introduction to this book.)

COLLECTION POINTS FOR EACH ORGAN

Collection Point for Kidneys (Bladder)

The collection point for the kidneys (and bladder) is at the perineum. A sphere approximately three inches (7.62 centimeters) in diameter is created at the perineum, which acts as a container for the kidneys' energy.

The energy of the kidneys is cold/wet in quality. The kidneys are associated with the winter season, the water element, and a deep blue color.

Collection Point for Heart/Thymus (Small Intestine)

The collection point for the heart/thymus (and small intestine) is located between the nipples (in men), or approximately one inch up from the bottom tip of the sternum (in women). A three-inch-diameter sphere is formed there to collect heart and thymus energy.

The heart's energy is hot, and its season is summer. Its element is fire, and its color is a bright red.

Collection Point for Liver (Gallbladder)

The collection point for the liver (and gallbladder) is located on the right side just below the rib cage and level with the navel. It is at the point of intersection of a vertical line mentally drawn down from the nipple and a line extending horizontally to the right side from the navel. A three-inch-diameter sphere is formed at this spot to collect the liver's energy.

The energy of the liver is warm and moist in quality. The liver is associated with the spring season. Its element is wood, and its color is bright green.

Collection Point for Lungs (Large Intestine)

The collection point for the lungs (and large intestine) is located on the left side just below the rib cage. It is level with the navel at the intersection of a line mentally drawn down from the nipple and a line extending across to the left side from the navel. A three-inch-diameter sphere is formed at this spot to collect the lungs' energy.

The energy of the lungs is cool and dry in quality. It is associated with the fall season, the element metal, and a radiant white color.

Collection Point for Spleen/Pancreas (Stomach)

The collection point for the spleen/pancreas (and stomach) is directly behind the navel (at the center of the front pakua). A three-inch-diameter sphere is formed at this spot to collect the spleen's energy.

The energy of the spleen is mild, and its season is Indian summer. Its element is earth, and its color is a brilliant golden yellow.

 ## Practice of Formula 2

To blend the organ energy, you first form the collection points for the kidneys and the heart. Then you blend the kidneys' (cold) energy with the heart's (hot) energy at the front pakua. Next, you form the collection points for the liver and the lungs, and then add and blend the liver's (warm, moist) and lungs' (cool, dry) energy at the front pakua. Finally, you add the spleen's (mild) energy gathered into its collection point located at the center of the front pakua.

Practice the Inner Smile

As you proceed with each step and smile to each organ, concentrate on the positive emotion associated with the organ. Sit up properly, hands together, and put the tongue up to the roof of the mouth. Smile down.

Form the Front Pakua

Form the front pakua as described in Formula 1, and feel the pakua glow with light.

Balance the Energies of the Kidneys and Heart: Form the Kidneys' Collection Point

1. Be aware of the kidneys.
2. Do the kidneys' sound: choo-oo-oo-oo (as when blowing out a candle). Practice a few times until you can feel the kidneys. (You

can review the "Six Healing Sounds" in *Chi Nei Tsang: Chi Massage for the Vital Organs* [Rochester, Vt.: Destiny Books, 2006].)

3. Using the Packing Process Breathing technique, slightly contract the left and right sides of the anus to squeeze the kidneys. Use the power of the mind rather than tension on the muscles to do this. Then release the contraction to sharpen your awareness. (To review the Packing Process Breathing technique, see *Iron Shirt Chi Kung* [Rochester, Vt.: Destiny Books, 2006].)

4. Form a sphere at the perineum, the kidneys' collection point, by inhaling, pulling up the perineum, and pushing the lower abdomen down to the perineum (fig. 2.1).

5. Exhale and relax. Mentally perceive the formation of a sphere and let it glow with a blue color.

6. Spiral the energy in both kidneys and in their collection point in either direction. Increase your awareness of the collection point and intensify the spiral there until you feel a force drawing the kidneys' (cold) energy into it.

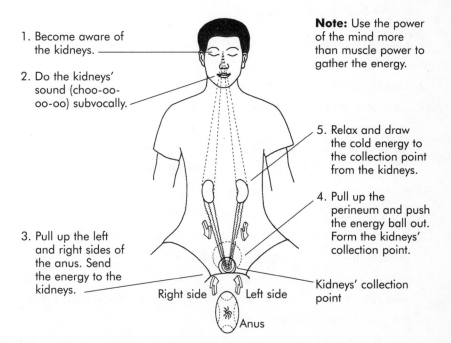

1. Become aware of the kidneys.

2. Do the kidneys' sound (choo-oo-oo-oo) subvocally.

3. Pull up the left and right sides of the anus. Send the energy to the kidneys.

Note: Use the power of the mind more than muscle power to gather the energy.

5. Relax and draw the cold energy to the collection point from the kidneys.

4. Pull up the perineum and push the energy ball out. Form the kidneys' collection point.

Kidneys' collection point

Right side   Left side

Anus

Fig. 2.1. Form the collection point to gather kidneys' energy.

☯ Form the Heart's Collection Point

1. Be aware of the heart and the thymus gland.
2. Do the heart's sound: haw-w-w-w-w-w.
3. Inhale and gently pull up the anus toward the heart, continuing to pull up until you feel the energy reach the heart. Then, using the power of the mind, gently squeeze or contract the heart area. Do not use too much physical force; it is better to use a gentle muscle contraction and the power of the mind.
4. Mentally perceive the formation of the sphere that is the heart's collection point. Let it glow with a red color.
5. Spiral the energy at the heart toward the heart's collection point. Intensify the spiral at the heart's collection point until the force of the spiral is strong enough to draw the hot energy of the heart and thymus into it.

☯ Spiral and Draw the Kidneys' and Heart's Energies to the Front Pakua

1. Divide your attention between the collection points of the kidneys and the heart.
2. Feel the cold and hot energy.
3. Also be aware of the front pakua. Spiral the kidneys' and heart's collection points and spiral the front pakua. Increase the spiraling force in the front pakua by using the eyes and the mind. Physically create a slight circling body movement at the same time to also help increase the spiraling force (fig. 2.2). Spiral until enough force is created to pull the cold (blue) energy (of the kidneys) and hot (red) energy (of the heart) into the front pakua. With each breath, inhale and draw up the cold, blue kidneys' energy to the pakua. Then exhale and draw down the hot, red heart's energy. Feel the energy blend. Moderate the temperature so that it is not too hot or too cold (fig. 2.3).

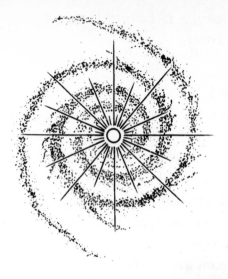

Fig. 2.2. Use the eyes, mind, and body to create a spiraling motion that will draw the energy into the spiral. Spiral until a pearl forms at its center. It was a spiral of energy that originally formed the universe.

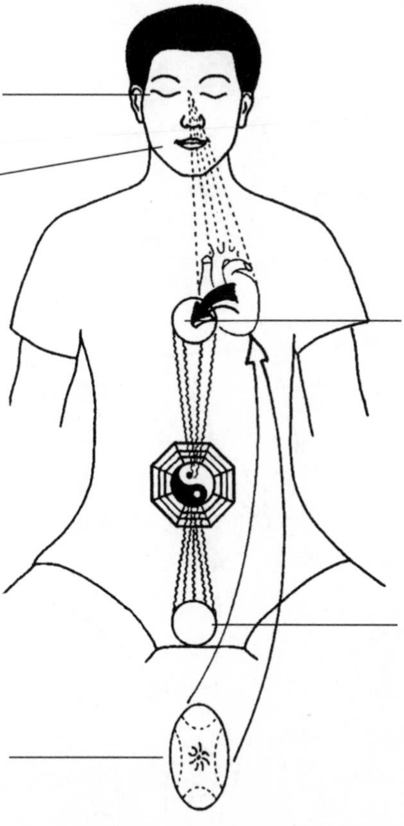

1. Become aware of the heart.

2. Do the heart's sound (haw-w-w-w-w-w) subvocally.

6. Use your mind and eyes to blend the hot and cold energies.

4. Pull the heart and thymus's energy into the heart's collection point.

5. Pull the heart energy down into the front pakua and pull the kidneys' energy up from the perineum into the front pakua.

3. Pull up the anus toward the heart and form the heart's collection

Fig. 2.3. Form the heart's collection point. Blend the heart's energy with kidneys' energy in the pakua.

☯ Balance the Energies of the Liver and Lungs: Form the Liver's Collection Point

1. Be aware of the liver.
2. Do the liver's sound: sh-h-h-h-h-h-h.
3. Inhale, and contract the right side of the anus to the liver. Then contract the liver.
4. Form the liver's collection point by inhaling, pulling up the right side of the anus, and pushing down on the right side of your body under the rib cage. Contract the muscles in this area.
5. Relax, and mentally perceive the formation of a bright green-colored sphere that is the collection point for the liver.
6. Spiral and draw the moist, warm liver energy into its collection point (fig. 2.4).

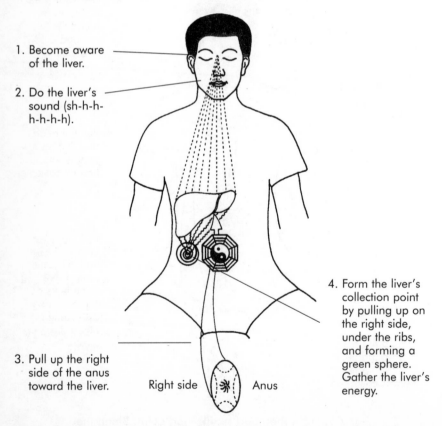

1. Become aware of the liver.

2. Do the liver's sound (sh-h-h-h-h-h).

3. Pull up the right side of the anus toward the liver.

Right side   Anus

4. Form the liver's collection point by pulling up on the right side, under the ribs, and forming a green sphere. Gather the liver's energy.

Fig. 2.4. Form the liver's collection point to gather the liver's energy.

⚫ Form the Lungs' Collection Point

1. Be aware of the lungs.
2. Do the lungs' sound: sss-s-s-s-s-s.
3. Inhale, pull up the left and right sides of the anus toward the lungs under the rib cage. Contract the lungs.
4. Form the lungs' collection point by inhaling again, pulling up the anus to the level of the navel, and mentally drawing a line down from the left nipple. Feel an expansion in this area.
5. Exhale, relax, and mentally perceive the formation of a metallic white, three-inch sphere under the left rib cage that is the collection point for the lungs.
6. Spiral and draw the dry, cool lungs' energy to its collection point (fig 2.5).

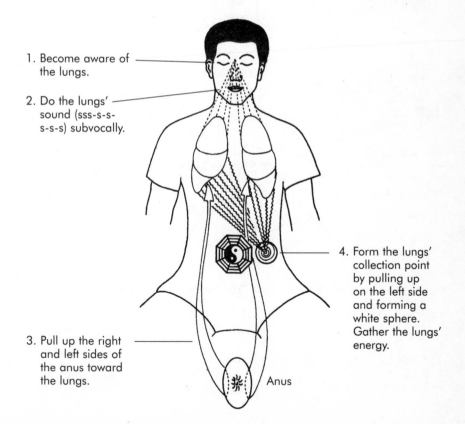

1. Become aware of the lungs.

2. Do the lungs' sound (sss-s-s-s-s-s) subvocally.

4. Form the lungs' collection point by pulling up on the left side and forming a white sphere. Gather the lungs' energy.

3. Pull up the right and left sides of the anus toward the lungs.

Anus

Fig. 2.5. Form the lungs' collection point to gather the lungs' energy.

☯ *Spiral and Draw the Liver's and Lungs' Energies to the Front Pakua*

1. Divide your attention between the collection points of the liver and the lungs, and spiral them both. Distinguish the warm, moist energy of the liver and the dry, cool energy of the lungs.
2. Be aware of the front pakua. Spiral and draw the liver's and lungs' energies into this pakua. Blend the energies so that they are not too warm and moist, nor too cool and dry (fig. 2.6).

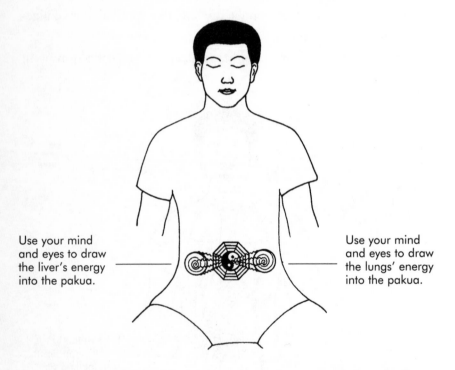

Use your mind and eyes to draw the liver's energy into the pakua.

Use your mind and eyes to draw the lungs' energy into the pakua.

Fig. 2.6. Blend the liver's and lungs' energies in the front pakua.

◑ *Pull the Spleen's Energy into the Front Pakua*

1. Be aware of the spleen on the left side, slightly toward the back.
2. Do the spleen's sound: who-o-o-o-o-o. Do this subvocally, but feel it in the vocal cords.
3. Inhale and pull up the left side of the anus toward the spleen. Use your mind to lightly squeeze the muscles on your back, and feel the spleen. Exhale, relax, and heighten your awareness of the spleen. Form the spleen's collection point, which is at the center of the front pakua itself.
4. Divide your attention between the spleen and the front pakua. Spiral and draw the spleen's mild energy into the pakua. Visualize the color yellow at the pakua (fig. 2.7).

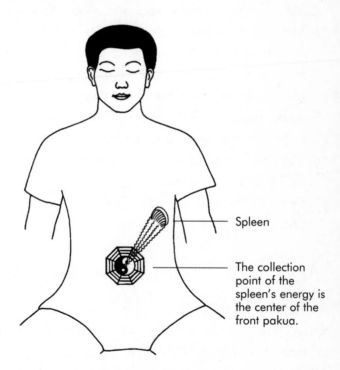

Spleen

The collection point of the spleen's energy is the center of the front pakua.

Fig. 2.7. Gather the spleen's energy directly into the pakua.

❷ Form the Back Pakua and Blend the Energy from the Back Collection Points

1. Form or copy the back pakua one and a half inches in from the Door of Life as described in chapter 1. When you have done so and definitely can perceive the back pakua, spiral and collect the energies from the following locations. (Note that the location of the collection points you will create now will not be the same as the designated organ collection points we have just described. Rather, they are located *near* the organ collection points, and their function is to draw in any remaining energies that may be present in the areas of the nearby organs. The actual source of these energies may be unclear.)
2. Make a sphere at the sacrum, and collect the kidneys' cold energy.
3. Make a sphere behind the heart between T5 and T6. Spiral and collect the heart's hot energy.
4. Spiral and blend the hot and cold energies that you have gathered from these spheres at the back pakua.
5. To the right rear of the back pakua, make a sphere. Spiral and collect the liver's warm, moist energy.
6. To the left rear of the back pakua, make a sphere. Spiral and collect the lungs' dry, cool energy.
7. Spiral and blend the energies of the right and left spheres into the back pakua (fig. 2.8).

❷ Draw the Energies from the Front and Back Pakuas into the Cauldron

Spiral, draw, and condense the energies from the front and back pakuas into the cauldron. Blend them together.

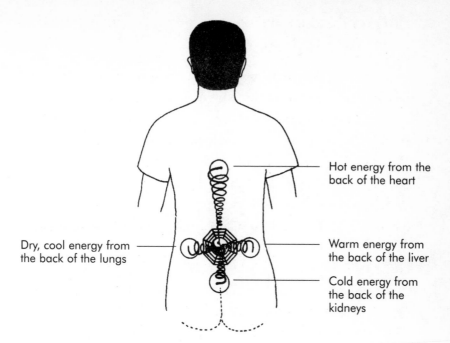

Fig. 2.8. Back pakua collection points

Form the Right Side Pakua and Blend the Energies from the Right Side Collection Points

1. Form the right side pakua. Spiral and draw energy from the following locations.
2. Form a sphere at the right hip, at the same level as the perineum. Spiral and draw any residual cold energy into the sphere.
3. Round the upper back like a turtle shell, to separate the scapulae and open the armpit, and create a sphere at the right armpit to collect residual hot energy.
4. Spiral and blend the hot and cold energies in the right side pakua.
5. Form a sphere toward the front of the right pakua. Spiral and collect residual warm, moist energy.

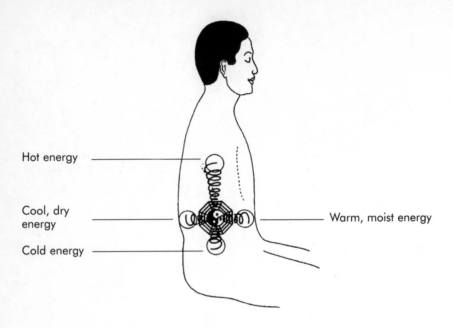

Hot energy

Cool, dry
energy

Cold energy

Warm, moist energy

Fig. 2.9. Right side pakua and its collection points

6. Form a sphere toward the back of the right pakua, and collect
   residual cool, dry energy.
7. Spiral and blend the warm, moist and cool, dry energies in the
   right side pakua (fig. 2.9).

Form the Left Side Pakua and Blend the Energies from the Left Side Collection Points

1. Form the left side pakua and draw energy from the following
   locations.
2. Form spheres, and collect the energies, at the left hip and armpit
   as described for the right side. Spiral and blend the hot and cold
   energies in the left pakua.

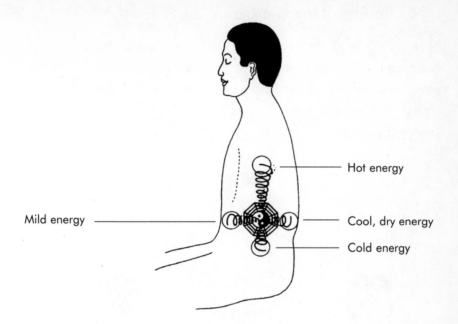

Mild energy

Hot energy

Cool, dry energy

Cold energy

Fig. 2.10. Left side pakua and its collection points

3. Form spheres to the front and back of the left pakua, as described for the right side. Spiral and collect mild energy at the front sphere. Spiral and collect cool, dry energy at the back sphere. Spiral and blend the mild and the cool, dry energies in the left pakua (fig 2.10).

❷ Draw the Energies from the Right and Left Pakuas into the Cauldron

1. Pull the energies now in the right and left side pakuas into the cauldron.
2. Spiral and blend them together with the energies already drawn there from the front and back pakuas.

⊙ Condense the Energies into a Refined Pearl

Now condense all the energies that you have pulled from the front, back, and side pakuas into a pearl. This pearl, created from the essence of your organs and your whole body, is very refined and not scattered. You may perceive it as a point of light or as condensed energy (fig. 2.11).

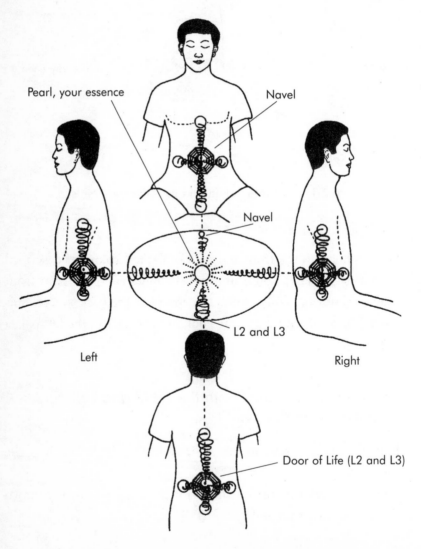

Fig. 2.11. Four pakuas and their collection points

◕ Anchor the Feelings of Peace and Harmony to the Pearl

At the height of feeling centered, at peace, and in inner harmony, anchor these feelings to the pearl by giving yourself a strong affirmation. For example: "I feel deeply centered and at peace, in inner harmony."

◕ Move the Pearl into the Microcosmic Orbit

Send the pearl down to the perineum, and circulate it in the Microcosmic Orbit. Be aware of the universal, cosmic particle, and earth forces as they are drawn to the pearl.

◕ Collect the Energy and Practice Chi Massage

Circulate the energy to the navel, and spiral it outward at the navel nine times (men should spiral clockwise, women, counterclockwise). Then, reverse and spiral it inward (men counterclockwise, women clockwise) six times. Rub your hands together, and practice Chi Massage. If you plan to continue without stopping at this point, you can spiral the energy at the navel and then continue on to the next chapter.

Formula 3

Connecting the Senses with the Organs, Controlling the Senses, Sealing the Openings, Overcoming Temptations

As a parent relates to a child, each of your senses relates to a specific organ. If, like undisciplined children, the organs expel negative energy, they need to be controlled or given balance and harmony by the senses, their parents. If either the senses or the organs are weak or sick, there will be no discipline and thus greater amounts of negative emotions will be created. By recognizing the parent/child relationships and strengthening them, you will be able to increase your energy.

CONNECTING THE SENSES WITH THE ORGANS

Ears—Kidneys

The ears are the openings of the kidneys. By increasing your awareness of and listening to the kidneys, you draw your sense of hearing within where it will eventually be controlled. You will eventually feel internal balance, peace, and harmony, since the ears will enable you to hear a heavenly music that is very unlike earthly music (fig. 3.1).

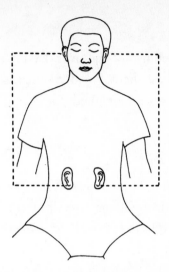

Fig. 3.1. Connect the ears with the kidneys.

Tongue—Heart

The tongue is the opening of the heart. By the awareness of connecting the tongue with the heart, you draw the speech center within, and there, the temptation of senseless speech can be controlled. The tongue and the heart will feel at peace (fig. 3.2).

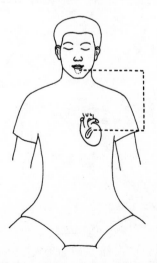

Fig. 3.2. Connect the tongue with the heart.

Eyes—Liver

The eyes are the openings of the liver. By looking into the liver and bringing your awareness there, you draw the sense of sight within, and visual temptations can be controlled (fig. 3.3).

Nose—Lungs

The nose is the opening of the lungs. When, with your awareness, you connect the nose with the lungs, you draw the sense of smell within, and the temptations of scents can be controlled (fig. 3.4).

Mouth—Spleen

The mouth is the opening of the spleen. By bringing your awareness to connecting the mouth with the spleen, you draw the sense of taste within, and the temptations of the appetite can be controlled (fig. 3.5).

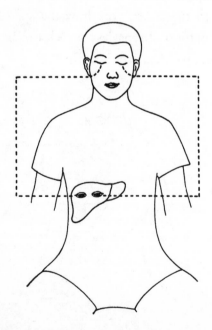

Fig. 3.3. Connect the eyes with the liver.

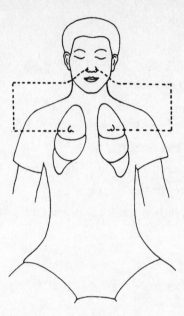

Fig. 3.4. Connect the nose with the lungs.

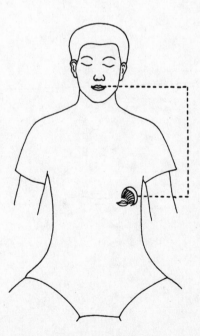

Fig. 3.5. Connect the mouth with the spleen.

Practice of Formula 3

You will connect each sense with its corresponding organ by connecting them in pairs (fig. 3.6).

1. The ears connect to the kidneys (cold energy) and the tongue to the heart (hot energy).
2. The eyes connect to the liver (warm/moist energy) and the nose to the lungs (cool/dry energy).
3. The mouth connects to the spleen (mild energy) and the front pakua.

☯ *Practice the Inner Smile and Chi Massage*

1. Sit up properly, hold the hands together, and press the tongue to the palate.
2. Smile down. Feel the energy flow down through the face to the

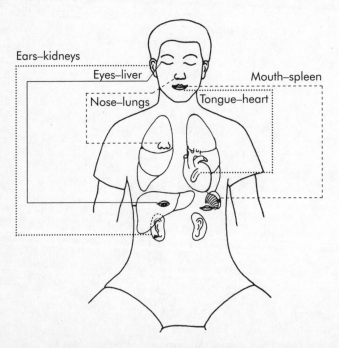

Fig. 3.6. Connections between the senses and the organs

organs. Feel the positive emotions in each organ. Smile to the navel, and form the front pakua.

3. You can massage the senses by practicing the Chi Self Massage exercise on them while massaging and exercising the organs. (For more information, see *Chi Self-Massage*.)

◉ Concentrate on the Ears and Kidneys

1. Concentrate on the ears by spiraling the energy there. Listen, turn your awareness inwardly to the kidneys, and direct the spiral you have created at the ears to the kidneys. With this connection, draw the essence of the ears to the kidneys by emphasizing the spiral at the kidneys, thereby making the energy at the kidneys stronger. Then collect, at the kidneys, the hearing energy of the ears and the cold energy that is the kidneys' essence.

2. Create a sphere at the perineum (the kidneys' collection point), and spiral at the perineum to draw and collect into this sphere the cold energy that is the kidneys' essence and the hearing energy that is the ears' essence (fig. 3.7).

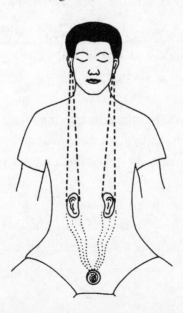

Fig. 3.7. Spiral and collect the ears and kidneys' energy.

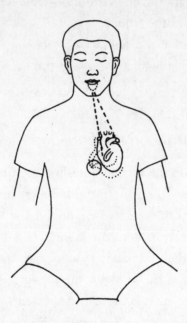

Fig. 3.8. Spiral and collect the tongue and heart's energy.

☻ Concentrate on the Tongue and Heart

1. Concentrate awareness on your tongue. Move the tongue around to generate saliva, and gently and carefully massage the heart. Spiral the energy at the tongue.

2. Swallow the saliva you have created, and spiral the tongue's essence toward the heart. Keeping this connection, turn your awareness toward the heart. Emphasize the spiral at the heart, and collect at the heart the tasting energy of the tongue and the hot energy that is the essence of the heart.

3. Make a sphere at the heart's collection point, and create a strong spiral there. Draw in and collect the hot energy that is the heart's essence and the tasting energy that is the tongue's essence (fig. 3.8).

◐ Spiral and Blend the Essence Energies in the Front Pakua

1. Spiral from the two collection points to the front pakua, and blend the energies from the kidneys and the heart. Feel the hot and cold essence energies blend together.
2. Notice the senses being pulled within.

◐ Concentrate on the Eyes and Liver

1. Concentrate awareness on the eyes. Move the eyes around, and massage the eyes and liver. Look inwardly to the liver, and make a connection between your eyes and your liver by spiraling between the eyes and the liver. Create a stronger spiral at the liver, and let it draw in the seeing energy of the eyes. Collect in the liver the moist, warm energy that is the liver's essence.
2. Make a sphere at the collection point below the liver. Spiral and collect the blended warm/moist energy of the liver's essence and the seeing essence of the eyes into this collection point (fig. 3.9).

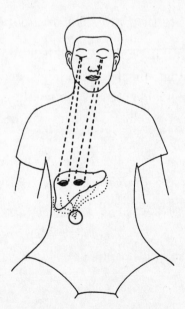

Fig. 3.9. Spiral and collect the eyes and liver's energy.

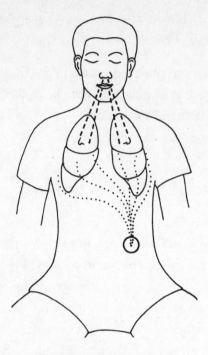

Fig. 3.10. Spiral and collect the nose and lungs' energy.

◐ Concentrate on the Nose and Lungs

1. Focus your attention on the nose. Inhale and exhale, and massage the nose and lungs. Inhale to the lungs, and feel the connection between the lungs and nose by spiraling the energy between them. Spiral and collect the dry/cool energy of the lungs and the smelling energy of the nose.

2. Make a sphere at the collection point below the left lung. Spiral and collect the dry/cool energy that is the lungs' essence and the smelling essence of the nose into the collection point (fig. 3.10)

☯ Blend the Essence Energies of the Eyes/Liver and Nose/Lungs in the Front Pakua

1. Concentrate on the front pakua. Spiral and blend the energies of the eyes/liver and nose/lungs from their collection points.
2. As you spiral, feel their moist/warm and dry/cold energy blend together at the front pakua. Feel the senses becoming increasingly focused.

☯ Concentrate on the Mouth and Spleen

Concentrate awareness on your mouth, and establish a connection with the spleen by spiraling between them. Collect the mild energy that is the essence of the spleen and the mouth in the front pakua. The senses should feel secure as the energies blend (fig. 3.11).

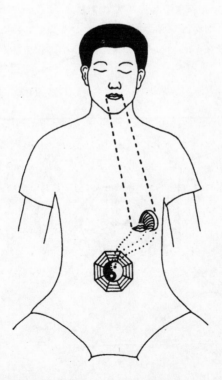

Fig. 3.11. Spiral and collect the mouth and spleen's energy.

🕹 Form the Back, Right, and Left Pakuas and Draw their Collected Energies into the Cauldron

1. Be aware of the back pakua, its collection points, and the energy that has been gathered. Spiral the front and back pakuas to draw into the cauldron, and combine their collected energies there, in the cauldron.
2. Be aware of the left pakua and its collection points. Similarly, be aware of the right pakua and its collection points.
3. Spiral the left and right pakuas to draw into the cauldron and combine their collected energies there (fig. 3.12).

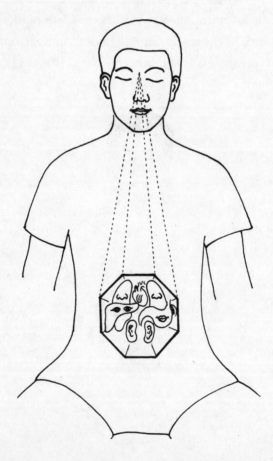

Fig. 3.12. Draw and combine the energies of all the senses
and organs in the cauldron.

☯ Form a Pearl

Spiral and blend all the condensed energies in the cauldron to form a pearl.

☯ Affirm your Self-Control: Anchor and Program the Pearl with Verbal Affirmations

Once you feel that the senses and organs are connecting and all energies are moving into one place—the cauldron—you will feel a sense of control. You will feel as though everything is under one roof or under one center of control. This feeling can make you stronger and increase your power to overcome temptations because your senses and organs will be stronger. At the height of the feeling of self-control, program yourself by anchoring this feeling into the pearl so that you can recall the feeling at any time. Tell yourself, "I am calm, clear, at peace, centered, in physical and emotional balance, and under self-control."

☯ Move the Pearl to the Perineum, Collect the Energy, and Practice Chi Massage

Move the pearl to the perineum and circulate the energy in the Microcosmic Orbit. Keep the senses and your awareness focused inward. As the pearl circulates in the Microcosmic Orbit, sense the three sources of energy that are supplying you: the universal, the cosmic particle, and the earth forces.

Bring the pearl of energy to the cauldron, and end with Chi Massage.

Formula 4

Transforming the Negative Emotions of Each Organ into Useful Energy

Taoists reason that negative emotions can be transformed to utilize their life-force energy. Therefore, to expel or suppress unwanted, negative emotions is to expel or suppress life force. Rather than suppress negative emotions in the Taoist system, you benefit more by experiencing them (fig. 4.1). This means you permit them to emerge but do not let them run wild or trigger other negative emotions. Instead, you put yourself in control of them so that you may transform them not only into useful life-force energy, but also into the higher consciousness that is your spiritual energy.

When connecting the senses with the organs in chapter 3, you may have noticed your emotions beginning to emerge. You can control them. Review Table 1 on page 66 to note the negative emotions you will want to transform. After you have learned Formula 4 and practiced clearing the negative emotions from the organs, review Table 2 on page 68. Table 2 gives details on the negative and positive aspects of each modality—shape, color, smell, temperature, and so forth. You may be stronger in one representational system than another, depending on your visual, auditory, and kinesthetic perceptions. You should be able to relate to at least one of the modalities.

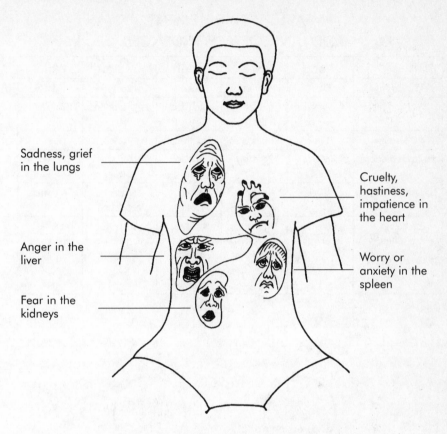

Sadness, grief in the lungs

Anger in the liver

Fear in the kidneys

Cruelty, hastiness, impatience in the heart

Worry or anxiety in the spleen

Fig. 4.1. Negative emotions and the organs

As we learn and proceed on through the more advanced Fusion practices, we will add more correspondences to the table showing the five element organ correspondences.

Some people have repressed their emotions and react strongly to this practice as their emotions surface. If you are one of these people, spend more time practicing the Healing Sounds and the Inner Smile. Work with healing the organs before attempting to transform the deeply buried emotions within them.

As you transform the negative emotions of each organ into useful energy, use the "counteracting or controlling cycle" to help balance the energy (see fig. 4.2 on page 66).

TABLE 1. FIVE ELEMENT
ORGAN CORRESPONDENCES

	Wood	Fire	Earth	Metal	Water
Yin organs	Liver	Heart	Spleen	Lungs	Kidneys
Yang organs	Gallbladder	Small intestine	Stomach, pancreas	Large intestine	Bladder
Openings	Eyes	Tongue	Mouth, lips	Nose	Ears
Positive emotions	Kindness	Love, joy	Fairness, openness	Righteousness, courage	Gentleness
Negative emotions	Anger	Hate, impatience	Worry, anxiety	Sadness, depression	Fear, stress
Psychological qualities	Control, decisiveness	Warmth, vitality, excitement	Ability to integrate, stabilize, center, and balance	Strength, substantiality	Ambition, willpower

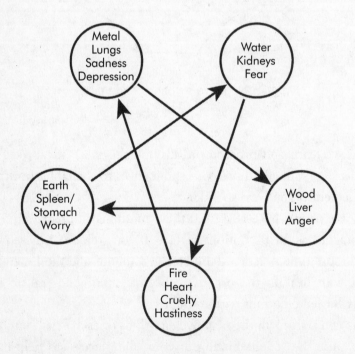

Fig. 4.2. The counteracting or controlling cycle

EMOTIONAL TRANSFORMATION PROCESSES

Table 2 on page 68 demonstrates emotional characteristics as they might be perceived by an individual. These are personal experiences, not elemental characteristics. Each person might feel differently according to his or her visual, auditory, and kinesthetic perceptions.

Practicing Inner Observation

When you turn the senses inward, you initiate the training process of inner observation. By developing the ability to focus inward—to smell, listen, taste, see, and hear the organs and their activities—and to observe your negative emotions without predetermined judgments, you have the opportunity to develop your true nature.

Cleaning Out the Negative Energy to make Room for Positive Energy

In the same way that turning garbage into compost makes it useful, transformed negative energy also becomes useful. You are increasing your life force rather than throwing it away. As you make room for positive energy to grow, your life force will continue to increase.

Allowing Virtue Energy to Grow in the Organs

Growing virtue energy is an essential part of both the Fusion I and II practices. Gentleness can grow in the kidneys. Love, happiness, and joy can grow in the heart. Kindness can grow in the liver. Righteousness and courage can grow in the lungs. Fairness and openness can grow in the spleen.

Check the color of each organ as a reflection of its increasing virtue energy. After learning and practicing the Fusion of the Five Elements, the kidneys might be a brilliant blue; the heart, a brilliant red; the lungs, a brilliant white; the liver, a brilliant green; and the spleen, a brilliant yellow. (See Table 2.)

TABLE 2. CHARACTERISTICS OF POSITIVE AND NEGATIVE EMOTIONS

	Lungs		Kidneys		Liver		Heart		Spleen	
Emotion	Sadness, grief	Righteousness, courage	Fear, stress, fright	Gentleness	Anger	Kindness	Impatience, cruelty, hate	Love, honor, respect	Worry	Fairness, openness
Shape	Collapsed, flattened ball	Tall, straight	Awkward, compressed	Round, full, expansive	Sharp, spearlike	Round, smooth	Moving, spiny	Straight, open	Irregular	Open, wide, big
Color	Gray	Bright white	Dark gray, cloudy	Bright sky blue	Red, cloudy	Soft green	Orange, muddy	Bright red	Cloudy	Mellow yellow
Smell	Musty	Pure, fresh	Foul, urine	Fresh	Pungent	Sweet, fragrant	Sharp, burnt	Aromatic incense	Sour	Clean, dry
Temperature	Cold	Comfortable, cool	Cold, chilly	Warm, comfortable	Hot, explosive	Warm, pleasant	Unsteady	Warm, full	Humid	Warm, balmy
Sound	Low, no force	Strong, firm, resonant	High-pitched, shrill	Whisper, pleasant to ear	Clashing, loud	Melodious	Noisy, irregular	Stable, steady, solid	Shaky	Clear, soft, in tune
Feeling	No energy, exhausted	Uplifted	Tight, closed in	Relaxed, high, centered	Painful, tough, rough	Nurtured	Irritated	Stable, protected	Uncertain	Balanced, even
Texture	Crumpled	Firm but comfortable	Slippery	Velvety	Rough	Soft	Cactuslike	Comforting, secure	Sticky	Smooth, firm
Size	Deflated, low	Expanding upward	Small	Limitless	Expand, explode	Expand, gently	Small, pointed	Expanding	Out of proportion	Big, deep
Taste	Salty	Satisfying	Salty	Mild honey	Bitter	Sweet	Acetic	Satisfying	Sour	Smooth, clean
Direction	Downward	Upward	Scattered	Circular	Attacking, outward	Enfolding	Scattered	Open, steady	Constricting	Horizontal

Organs made stronger with the growth of virtue energy will gradually strengthen the senses. During the process, you will develop a very real sense of knowledge and true wisdom. Once you observe these qualities within yourself, you are prepared to observe and experience the outside world.

Transforming the Negative Energy as the Most Powerful Act of Forgiveness

Recall a time when you had a conflict or argument with someone. Finally there came a time when you both sat down to talk things over and to try to understand each other. You said, "I forgive you," and the other person also forgave. At that moment the feeling was as though a heavy load or burden was removed. You felt open, happy, and warm.

When you can transform anger into kindness, you are performing the act of forgiveness. Forgiveness is one of the most important practices of the Taoist system. Feel the anger of others. Do not suppress it. Do not be afraid of it. Make friends with it. Understand it and draw its energy into your pakua. Spiral it with your other emotions and add more of your love energy. Transform the combined energies into life force.

At the moment the energy transforms into life force, you feel a sense of release, a sense of opening. Experience the feeling. Remember that it will help you to transform more energy easily.

Projecting Inner Virtue Outward to Increase Virtue Energy

The Taoist way emphasizes helping the world without anyone noticing. Once you have grown love, joy, kindness, and gentleness internally, it can be projected outward toward others. The more virtue energy you project outwardly, the more you grow inwardly. The more you give, the more you receive without ever asking for reward.

You can help sad and angry people with your good virtue. Extend your help to them daily and you will touch their hearts with love, joy, and kindness. You, in turn, will feel the universal force pouring out from the heavens. The New Testament of the Bible relates a narrative of Jesus regarding donations to the temple. He told us not to let the left hand know what the right hand gives. It is only for the Heavenly Father to know.

As the organ virtue energy increases, it becomes useful energy for transforming your consciousness. Therefore, it becomes valuable for all eternity. The consciousness created and transformed by virtue energy can be thought of as money in a savings account, an account held by the universe.

Practicing External Observation and Developing the Art of Non-Attachment

Another important Taoist discipline to realize at this time is the art of non-attachment to the material and social elements of your physical world. It is an important concept to embrace when observing the outside world because it prepares you for your destiny.

Regard the necessities of life—food, clothing, shelter—simply as vehicles to help you reach your goal. Try to walk through your home, for example, and determine what it is possible to live without. Would you feel deprived if suddenly all your material things were taken away? If you were abandoned by your loved ones, would you be able to carry on?

The fact is that when, through death, you finally leave this world, you cannot take anything with you. The spirit is all that survives.

Preparing the Body to Receive the Universal Force

Clearing out negative emotions and blockages is important for another reason—to prepare the body and make room to receive the higher universal force and a higher consciousness. The universal force supplies useful energy for healing, for spiritual work, and for working on new projects when you require additional life-force energy to make decisions or to solve a crisis.

You might think of the process as "cleaning the house" to make it ready. This means you try to feel clean internally. The first step is to clean all the "rooms"; that is, to clear the negative energies from the organs. Next, it is particularly important to "clean the bathroom." This means to clear the intestines, especially the large intestine, since constipation is a serious prevention to the flow of energy. Consume a higher-fiber diet, including fruits and vegetables, to keep the body clean.

A clean "house" makes you feel very good, internally and externally. You feel as though you know yourself better. You are better able to determine your weak and strong points. The Fusion practices help you to replace automatically your weak points with stronger points. They also help you to control the overly strong ones. When you feel this strength and control, you will feel clean inside. This feeling of cleanliness is very important because it opens you up to attract and receive the higher force.

After your Fusion practice, and before you go to sleep, feel the clean feeling and the emptiness it creates inside. At this time ask the universe, with a good heart and in a virtuous way, for what you need to fill the emptiness. The universe will fill your need. When you arise in the morning, get in touch with yourself and any problem you may have, and you might find the answer has already arrived.

Increasing the Psychological Qualities of the Organs

The Taoists regard the organs as storage places for general information and data, while the brain uses this stored information and data for processing. You might consider this process to work much like the operation of a computer. The organs are like the software, and the brain is like the computer hardware. Without the software to feed information and data, the computer would not be able to exercise its function (see fig. 4.3 on page 72).

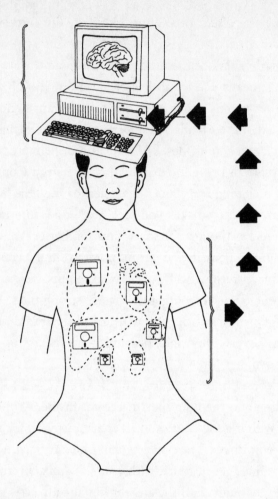

Fig. 4.3. The brain is the computer; the organs are the software.

Once you recognize this connection, you can understand the brain's function in strengthening and activating the advantageous psychological qualities of the organs, after they have been cleared of their negative energies.

Good psychological qualities associated with the organs are as follows:

- The kidneys and bladder—ambition and willpower
- The heart and small intestine—warmth, vitality, and excitement

- The liver and gall bladder—control and decisiveness
- The lungs and large intestine—strength and substantiality
- The spleen and the stomach—ability to integrate, stabilize, and feel centered and balanced. (See Table 1 on page 66.)

The lungs are associated with the element of metal. A person influenced by anger, sadness, and depression, negative emotions of the lungs, can experience a weakened liver. The liver is counteracted and controlled by the energy of the lungs, the metal element. A weakened liver will encourage anger and affect decision making. An extremely angry person will make wrong decisions. A person who is sad and depressed can lose both courage and a clear viewpoint. A hasty, impatient person, experiencing the negative emotions of the heart, can lose warmth and vitality.

By cleaning negative emotions from the organs and transforming them to positive energy, you are able to experience the vitality of the organs' positive psychological qualities. These good psychological qualities play a major role in our daily life, providing decision-making capabilities, sound judgment, and a sense of direction.

The Taoists believe that clean organs, emptied of their negative energies, permit good sense and real knowledge to come forth. Otherwise you can harbor a false knowledge that confuses real knowledge and good sense.

When Taoists say they feel fine, this means all the organs are in agreement, working together in a positive way and controlling all actions. They are free of domination by the mind.

Practice of Formula 4

◔ Practice the Inner Smile and Form the Front Pakua

Smile down, and feel the energy flow as you generate the qualities of loving energy in each organ. When you are ready, create the front pakua as in previous chapters.

☢ Be Aware of Fear in the Kidneys

1. Turn your consciousness toward your ears, and listen to the kidneys. Become aware of fear or any sensation that you do not like, as it manifests in the form of a sound, taste, color, shape, or feeling. The energy may be chilling and cold, cloudy blue, or contracting, or it may be emitting awkward shapes.
2. Spiral and breathe the fear and any other emotion you do not like out of the kidneys, and collect it at the kidneys' collection point (fig. 4.4).

☢ Be Conscious of Impatience in the Heart

1. Move the tongue, use your awareness to connect the tongue with the heart, and become conscious of impatience, hastiness, cruelty, or any sensation that you do not like deep within the heart. It may

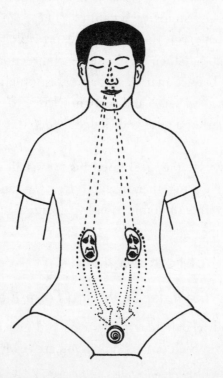

Fig. 4.4. Collecting fear in the kidneys' collection point

manifest as a feeling, shape, sound, or image. You might feel it as energy rushing out, and you might see and feel something wrapping and pressing in a bad way into the heart. You can sense the negative feelings of the heart as a very muddy, red color, or they can be hot, unsteady, small, noisy, or acidic.

2. Spiral and breathe these emotions out of the heart, and collect them at the heart's collection point (fig. 4.5).

◎ Spiral, Blend, and Transform the Energy of the Heart and Kidneys at the Front Pakua

1. Spiral and breathe the negative energies out from the collection points of the heart and kidneys to the front pakua. Spiral and blend them at the front pakua. The pure energy trapped in these negative feelings will be freed and released to the center of the pakua.

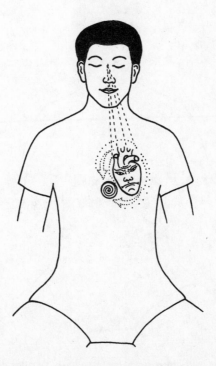

Fig. 4.5. Collecting cruelty, hastiness, and impatience
in the heart's collection point

2. Spiral the heart's and kidneys' energies until they become a bright, golden energy. This energy radiates love and gentleness from the center of the pakua and of your being.

☾ Perceive Anger in the Liver

1. Move your eyes, make the connection of the eyes with the liver, and be aware of anger or any sensation that you do not like deep within the liver. You can sense the anger energy as a sharp-edged spear, hot, painful, red, cloudy, or pungent. It can be a destructive, expanding kind of energy.
2. Spiral the anger and any other energy you do not like from the liver, and move it out to the liver's collection point (fig. 4.6).

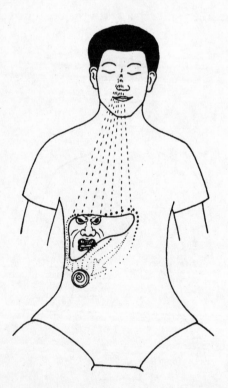

Fig. 4.6. Collecting anger in the liver's collection point

🌀 *Be Aware of Sadness and Depression in the Lungs*

1. Inhale and exhale. Then inhale again, and establish the connection between the nose and lungs. The negative energy of the lungs can take the form of sadness, grief, and depression, but it can be represented by other sensations that you do not like. When you are sad, you can have a sense of being down, collapsed, deflated, and low in energy. Sadness or any negative energy in the lungs can be gray, cold, musty, or salty.

2. Spiral and breathe out the sadness and any other energy you do not like from the lungs. Bring it to the lungs' collection point (fig. 4.7).

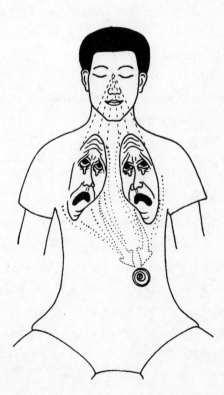

Fig. 4.7. Collecting sadness and grief in the lungs' collection point

◷ Spiral, Blend, and Transform the Energy of the Liver and Lungs at the Front Pakua

1. Spiral and breathe the negative emotional energies from the collection points of the liver and lungs to the front pakua.
2. Spiral and blend them at the front pakua, using the power of the pakua to balance and neutralize the sadness and anger. Nurturing the kindness and courage will help to transform them into a golden light at the center of the pakua.

◷ Be Conscious of Worry in the Spleen

1. Through your awareness, connect the mouth with the spleen, and be aware of worry or any other emotion you do not like in the spleen. You can sense the negative energy of the spleen as cloudy, sour, shaky, uncertain, and sticky. As a result, you might feel limited, small, and uneasy.
2. Spiral and breathe the worry and any other energy you do not like out of the spleen. Bring it to the front pakua to blend it with the energy that is already there (fig. 4.8).

◷ Spiral All Remaining Negative Energy to the Front Pakua

1. Return to all the organs and their collection points, and spiral and breathe to draw out any remaining negative energy. Blend and neutralize it with the energy in the front pakua.
2. If you feel you do not have enough energy to transform the negative emotions, you can call upon another source of energy within you to help. Become aware of the love and joy in your heart. Bring these emotions into the pakua, and they will help transform the negative energy.

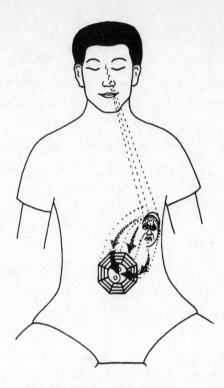

Fig. 4.8. Collecting worry and anxiety in the spleen's collection point

⊙ Form the Back, Right, and Left Pakuas and draw their Collected Energies into the Cauldron

1. Be aware of the back pakua, its collection points, and all the energies you have collected from the connected senses and organs.
2. Spiral the front and back pakuas to draw in and combine their collected energies into the cauldron. Be aware of the left pakua, its collection points, and all of the energies gathered there. Similarly, be aware of the right pakua, its collection points, and all of the energies now present there.
3. Spiral the left and right pakuas to draw in and combine their collected energies into the cauldron.

⊘ Form a Pearl

Fuse together and condense the energies from all four pakuas in the cauldron, and form a pearl. With the addition of the organs' and purified emotions' energies, the pearl now glows a brilliant golden color.

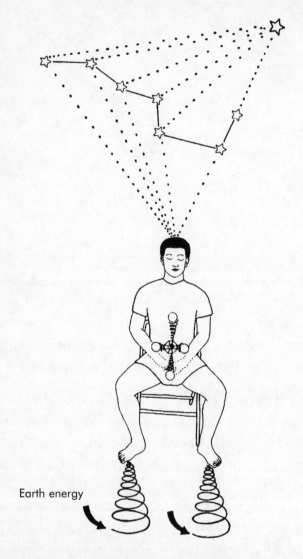

Earth energy

Fig. 4.9. Once you have established the energies in all four pakuas and begin circulating the Microcosmic Orbit, simply be aware of the earth force, the universal force, and the forces of the North Star and Big Dipper.

❷ Circulate the Pearl in the Microcosmic Orbit and Practice Chi Massage

Bring the pearl down to the perineum. Circulate it in the Microcosmic Orbit. As the pearl moves through the Microcosmic Orbit, feel the universal forces, the cosmic particle forces, and the earth forces that are supplying you (fig. 4.9).

Collect the energy and practice Chi Massage.

Formula 5

Creating the Pearl that Forms the Energy Body

Formula 5 incorporates Formulas 1 through 4 of Fusion I, and then continues to draw more energy into specific pakuas. The additional energies that you have brought to the front and back and the left and right pakuas are blended together. Then they are pulled into and condensed in the cauldron to create a more powerful pearl. The greatly refined and radiant energy of this pearl will be used to grow your soul or energy body.

Practice of Formula 5 to Create the Pearl

Practice the Inner Smile and Form the Front Pakua

Smile down, and feel the smiling energy flowing to the organs. Create the front pakua and see it glowing, using what you have learned in chapters 1 through 4.

Blend the Energy from the Front Collection Points

Connect the senses to the organs, collect the energy in the organs' collection points, and blend the organs' energies and emotions in the front pakua. Begin with the energies of the kidneys and heart, then blend the energies of the liver and lungs, and follow with the spleen's energies (fig 5.1).

❷ Form the Back, Right, and Left Pakuas and Draw their Collected Energies into the Cauldron

1. Be aware of the back pakua, its collection points, and all the energies you have collected from the connected senses and organs.
2. Spiral the front and back pakuas to draw the energies into the cauldron, and combine their collected energies there.
3. Be aware of the left pakua, its collection points, and all of the energies gathered there. Similarly, be aware of the right pakua, its collection points, and all of the energies now present there. Spiral the left and right pakuas to draw the energies into the cauldron, and combine their collected energies there.

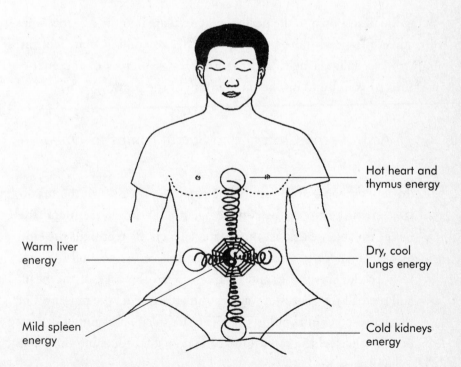

Fig. 5.1. Front pakua collection points

◯ Condense the Energies into a Refined Pearl

Fuse together the energies from all four pakuas in the cauldron and condense them there, to form the purified pearl of a brilliant, golden color.

Working with the Pearl

Practicing with the pearl is a very advanced procedure. For some, it may take a long time simply to create one. Do not rush—impatience will dissolve your pearl. You must master each of the following stages before going on to the next. (Such mastery becomes especially important when working with the pearl above the crown in the Fusion II practice.)

◯ Circulate the Pearl in the Microcosmic Orbit

Bring the pearl down to the perineum. Circulate it in the Microcosmic Orbit. As the pearl moves through the Microcosmic Orbit, feel the universal, cosmic particle, and earth forces as sources of the energy supplied to you. Build up the momentum of the pearl.

◯ Activate the Cranial and Sacral Pumps to Open the Crown

1. To activate the cranial pump (the palatine processes of the maxillae), press the tip of the tongue against the lower teeth and the flat of the tongue against the palate. Clench the teeth, tilt the chin toward the neck to straighten the cervical vertebrae, pull the eyes in, turn the ears, nose, and tongue toward the back of the head, and turn all the senses upward to the crown. Feel the pulsation of the activated cranial pump (fig. 5.2). (If you are a beginner, it may be easier to feel the pulsation at the crown by touching the pulse at your wrist.)

Note: Use the power of the mind more than muscle power to activate the cranial pump.

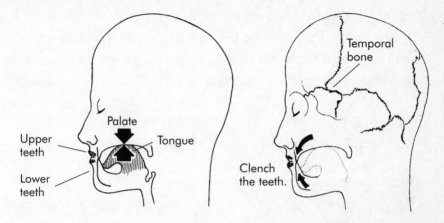

1. Press the flat part of the tongue against the palate.

2. Clench the teeth to activate the temporal bone.

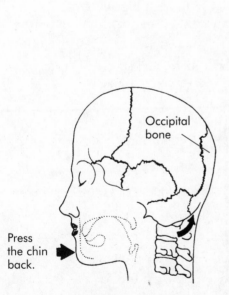

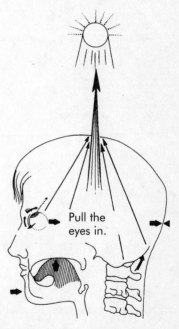

3. Tuck the chin toward the back to activate the occipital bone.

4. Pull the eyes into their sockets. Roll the eyes up and look up to the crown. Turn all the other senses upward toward the crown, as well.

Fig. 5.2. Activating the cranial pump

2. To activate the sacral pump, inhale, pull up the perineum, then inhale again, and pull up the back of the anus toward the sacrum. Inhale more, and pull the pearl from the perineum to the sacrum, up to T11, C7, the base of the skull, and the crown. Inhale once again, and feel the force at the crown (fig. 5.3). At this moment you might feel a strong sensation, like a shiny wave of light, called the lead light, emerge from the crown.

   If you suffer from heart disease or have difficulty breathing, hold your breath only as long as you feel comfortable.

3. Inhale, and swallow your saliva. This action will help you push the pearl upward toward the crown.

4. Feel the crown open.

5. Be aware of the crown and its opening. Swallow the saliva upward and feel a push up to the crown. Exhale forcefully toward the crown, and shoot the pearl out through the crown to approximately six inches (15.24 centimeters) above the head. When your practice is more advanced, you can move it higher.

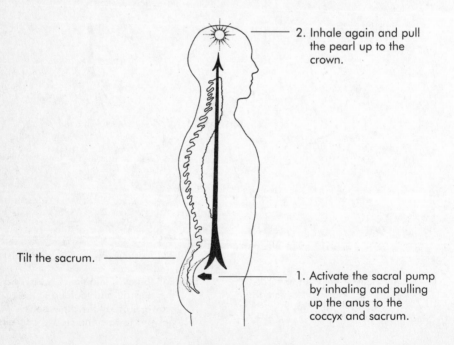

2. Inhale again and pull the pearl up to the crown.

Tilt the sacrum.

1. Activate the sacral pump by inhaling and pulling up the anus to the coccyx and sacrum.

Fig. 5.3. Activating the sacral pump

Look for the Lead Light

The lead light is the guiding light that you can feel through the crown. When, in the advanced stages of practice, you send the pearl out from the body to form the energy body, the light can be used by the energy body to communicate with the physical body. It can also be used as a compass to guide the energy body into the next world (fig. 5.4).

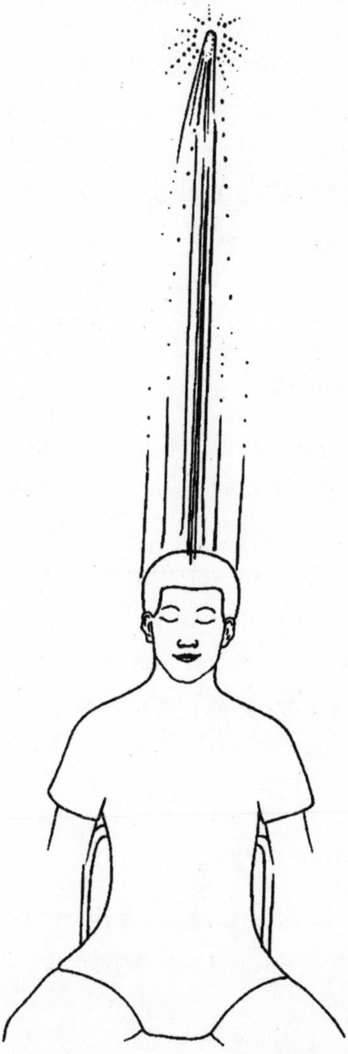

Fig. 5.4. The lead light

⟳ Extend the Pearl above the Crown

1. The senses now become the wireless control of the pearl. Begin by concentrating on moving the pearl up and down.
2. As you gain greater control, move it around in other directions.

⟳ Reactivate the Cranial Pump and Draw the Pearl Back into the Body's Microcosmic Orbit

1. Inhale and reactivate the cranial pump.
2. When the crown is open, inhale, and bring the pearl back into the Microcosmic Orbit.
3. Collect the energy in the navel and bring it to the cauldron.
4. Finish with Chi Massage.

⟳ Advanced Stage: Controlling the Pearl above the Physical Body

Move the pearl up in increments of one foot (30.48 centimeters) at a time, and practice until you have mastered control of the pearl at that level. Ultimately, you can bring the pearl up to a level equal to the height of your body. At each level, first move the pearl up and down, then experiment with different directions: left and right, front and back. Then spiral it to the left and the right, fast and slow, and so on. Once you have reached a certain proficiency at moving the pearl at one level, continue to the next (fig. 5.5).

⟳ Finish the Practice

You can finish your practice now, or continue to the next exercise. If you decide to finish now, you can reactivate the cranial pump and condense the pearl again.

1. Inhale, pull the pearl in through the cranial pump, and circulate it in the Microcosmic Orbit.

Fig. 5.5. Controlling the pearl above the physical body

2. Collect the energy in the navel, bring it to the cauldron, and finish
   with Chi Massage.

CREATING THE YIN AND YANG BODIES (SOUL AND SPIRIT BODIES) FOR SPACE TRAVEL

The new chi body that you will create in this chapter is known as your
energy or soul body, the body that will last forever. Most people are
afraid of death, but they need not be. The Taoist belief is that death
is the spirit changing residence. Your physical body will return to the
dust from which it came, but chi, soul, and spirit come from the planets and stars and from the Original Source, the Wu Chi. In separating
the soul and spirit from the physical body, you are practicing death
and your return to the Wu Chi. When you learn how to condense and
transfer this energy, and send it back to the planets and stars and to the

Original Source, you can be assured that your energy will continue as part of the universe.

During the course of a few thousand years of developing the energy and spirit bodies, the Taoists realized that the process could not be rushed. Developing the soul and spirit bodies is similar to taking care of a newborn infant. The infant needs to be nourished and cared for. As he or she grows up, the child needs to be educated and trained to the fullest potential. The child also needs to be equipped with the power to protect himself or herself.

The early, undeveloped stage in the creation of the energy body was regarded by the Taoists as the yin body or infant stage. In this infant stage, you do not let your energy body roam about without control, just as you would not allow a baby to crawl around unsupervised.

With practice, you can gradually change the yin body into more of a yang body. The transformation into a yang body is initiated by a transference of consciousness. The process begins in this chapter of Fusion I with the transference of the Microcosmic Orbit into the energy or soul body. The process continues with the practice of Fusion II and III, in which the virtue energies from the organs, the Belt Channel, the Thrusting Channels, and other channels are extended from the yin physical body up into the energy body. During this process the soul takes on a yang quality. As your practice continues, a spirit body is formed that is also a yang body, capable of traveling in space and capable of self-care.

THE PURPOSE OF TRAVELING IN SPACE

The main goal of your practice with the Universal Tao is to travel to a higher plane of energy.

The energy needed for absorption that helps develop the soul and spirit bodies is not available on the human plane. By traveling to a higher plane of energy, you are practicing your return to the Wu Chi, the Original Source from which you came.

In space traveling, the combined soul and spirit bodies you have developed can travel very fast. The speed is believed to be faster than the speed of light. It now becomes possible to encounter the souls and spirits of people who already have passed from their human lives. Some people travel to a different time, such as the time before they were born into their Earth lives. This ability also enables them to see into the future.

In Taoism and other systems, practitioners try to avoid those elements that in the past or future comprise their Earthly lives. Their aim is to try to return to the place of their origin, a place they would like to be. If, as in normal traveling on Earth, you continuously stop to talk to people, it will take much longer to arrive at your destination, or you may never arrive at all.

 ## How to Develop the Energy Body

The energy body is created by using the pearl. You can continue to use the pearl you have already developed, or, if you are starting fresh, create a pearl by practicing chapters 1 through 5 again.

Use a Pearl to Create the Energy Body

1. Circulate the pearl in the Microcosmic Orbit. Feel the forces supplying you with energy, and build up the momentum of the pearl.
2. Inhale, activate the cranial and sacral pumps, and shoot the pearl through the crown of the physical body. Bring the pearl to a level above and equal to the height of your physical body.

Create the Energy Body

1. Relax the senses and the mind, and then use them to expand the pearl (see fig. 5.6 on page 92). Begin to shape the pearl into a form similar to your own body, or into the image you would like your body to have. Initially it might feel like a great mass of

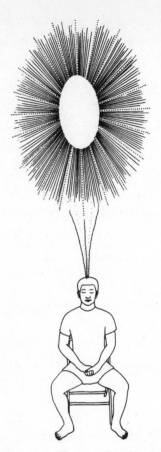

Fig. 5.6. Relax the senses and
mind; let the pearl expand.

Fig. 5.7. The pearl might feel
like a great mass of energy.

energy (fig. 5.7). Use your senses like carving tools to shape the
head, body, hands, and legs (fig. 5.8).

If you prefer a religious conceptualization, your goal may be
to form the image in the likeness of God, or perhaps the founder
of your religion, such as Buddha. Taoists believe all humans are
built in the image of God, since all people come from the Original
Source.

2. Once you sense the body is in good shape, use your senses again
to carve the face.

• To form the eyes, focus on the eyes of the physical body. When

Fig. 5.8. Continue expanding the pearl into an energy body.

you feel a very strong awareness of these eyes, condense their essence into a ball. Activate the crown, and exhale the ball to the place on the face of the energy body where the eyes will be positioned. Feel and affirm that the eyes of the energy body have been formed (see fig. 5.9 on page 94).

- Be aware of the physical ears. When you feel the essence of your physical body's ears is condensed into an energy ball, transfer it to the energy body's ears (see fig. 5.10 on page 94).

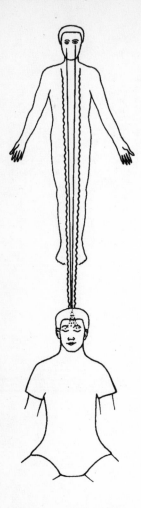

**Fig. 5.9. Forming the
energy body's eyes**

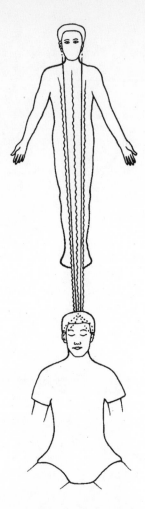

**Fig. 5.10. Forming the
energy body's ears**

- Be aware of the nose, and, in a similar way, transfer it up to the energy body (fig. 5.11).
- Be aware of the mouth, and similarly transfer it up to the energy body (fig. 5.12).
- Be aware of the tongue, and also transfer it up to the energy body.

3. Now you can form and arrange the senses of the energy body into shapes you like. You can make the nose longer or higher on the

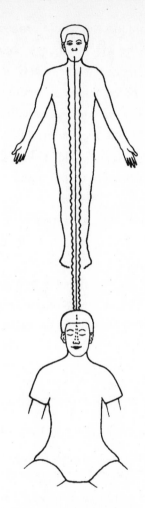

Fig. 5.11. Forming the
energy body's nose

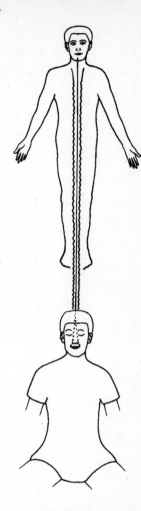

Fig. 5.12. Forming the
energy body's mouth

face, the eyes smaller or bigger, or the mouth wider or smaller.

4. Copy the cauldron within the physical body to the energy body by first concentrating on it. When you feel the energy is very condensed, shoot it up through the perineum of the energy body.

5. Now you can make the energy body the sex of your choice.

6. When you feel the energy body is fully grown, or formed into a very sharp image, you can give it an inner name and associate this name with it in the future. Then, in later practice, you will be able

to simply call the name of the energy form, and the whole process will take place instantly. It is best to keep the soul or energy body name to yourself, so that you will be the only one who can activate it. This is important, because in more advanced stages of practice, a person with bad intentions who knows your soul name could activate it and make use of it. That person could steal energy from your energy body, or tell the soul to do something that is bad. If this happens to you, you will have to change to a new name or code for your energy body.

7. In addition to associating the energy body with an inner name, you can also associate the energy body with an inner voice or inner voices. The inner voice (or voices) will give you advice to help you make decisions. The more you listen to the voice(s), the clearer it (or they) will become. As you begin to develop more virtue energy, the voice(s) will become more distinct. This will help you make choices between good and bad, help you to choose friends, and so on.

◎ Transfer the Microcosmic Orbit to the Energy Body

The energy body is a chi body that offers no resistance, and so it is very easy to open its Microcosmic Orbit. Creating the energy body and transferring the Microcosmic from the physical body to the energy body is the first transference of consciousness you will experience in your practice.

Each day as you work on this stage of Fusion, you transfer more consciousness to the energy body. At this stage, the energy body is simply a powerful projection of your mind and your physical body. At higher levels of practice, this energy body is crystallized into a permanent spiritual body.

1. Create another pearl in the cauldron and circulate it in the Microcosmic Orbit of the physical body.
2. Inhale, activate the cranial and sacral pumps, activate the lead light, and aim the lead light at the perineum of the energy body.

Shoot this pearl through the crown of the physical body and penetrate the perineum of the energy body.

3. Use the senses to move the pearl up to the energy body's sacrum. Stop for a while and feel the pearl establish itself at the sacrum point. Then move the pearl up to the Door of Life, T11, C7, base of the skull, crown, third eye, tongue, throat, heart, solar plexus, navel, sexual center, and perineum, completing the Microcosmic Orbit of the energy body. Another way to transfer the Microcosmic Orbit is simply to copy the Microcosmic of the physical body (fig. 5.13).

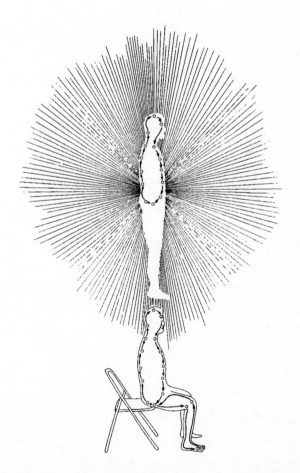

Fig. 5.13. Shoot the pearl to the perineum of the energy body to open its Microcosmic Orbit. Circulate both Microcosmic Orbits.

◎ Form a Protective Shield around the Energy Body

1. Form another pearl in the physical body, and circulate it in the Microcosmic Orbit of the physical body until it gains momentum.
2. Once it has gained momentum, and upon its return to the perineum of the physical body, begin to move the pearl up again through the physical body, as follows. Inhale and activate the cranial pump. Contract the perineum, the anus, and the back of the anus. Pull the pearl up to the sacrum, the Door of Life, T11, C7, the base of the skull, and toward the back of the crown to a point about one and a half inches behind the crown. Hold at this point.
3. Feel the pulsation at the back of the crown. Exhale and shoot the pearl out. Use the pearl to form a bubble to cover the entire energy body.

◎ Form a Great Bubble to Encase Both Bodies in a Protective Shield

1. Form one more pearl. Circulate this pearl in the Microcosmic Orbit of the physical body to gain momentum. Stop again at the perineum of the physical body.
2. As above, pull the pearl all the way up the Governor Channel of the physical body to the point one and a half inches behind the crown. Shoot it out from this point to encircle the energy body, bringing it all the way down to cover the physical body as well. You now have formed a great bubble encasing both bodies and the protective shield of the energy body (fig. 5.14).
3. Be aware of the energy body, the physical body, and the bubbles that form the protective shields around both bodies. Also be aware of the energy above the energy body and below the physical body.

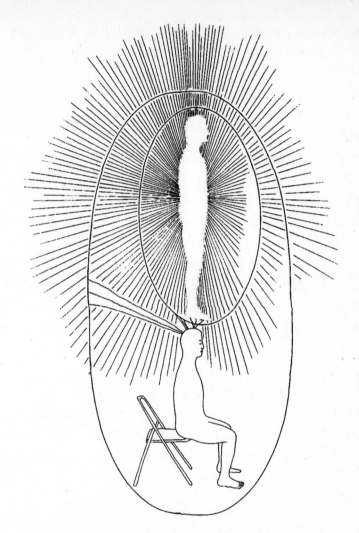

Fig. 5.14. Form an energy body, its protective shield,
and a great bubble to protect all.

☯ Draw in the Energy Body and the Big Protective Bubble to Finish the Practice

1. When you are ready to finish this practice, first absorb as much as possible of the heavenly force once more.
2. Condense the energy body back into a pearl, drawing in the energy through the energy body's navel, still surrounded by the

bubble that serves as its protective shield. Notice that the color of the pearl may now be brighter, or the pearl may have grown larger.

3. Be aware of the big bubble that continues to protect the physical and energy bodies, and the energy body's bubble, as a great protective shield.

4. Inhale and activate the cranial pump. Feel the pulsation. Feel the lead light extend out from the crown point.

5. Inhale and slowly use the mind and senses to draw in the pearl. Inhale again and use your mind to guide the pearl to land on the opening of the crown where the lead light emerges. Inhale once more with force to pull the pearl down from the crown through the front channel.

6. Circulate the pearl in the Microcosmic Orbit. As the enhanced pearl moves around the Orbit, it will bring its heightened energy to the organs and glands. Any part of the body that requires it will absorb it.

7. Be aware of the energy body's protective bubble remaining above the physical body and within the big protective bubble. Be aware of the crown and the point one and a half inches behind the crown. Inhale and draw the energy body's bubble through the crown and the back of the crown into the Microcosmic Orbit, and add this energy to the pearl that is already circulating.

   The energy that now circulates in the Microcosmic Orbit is the combined energy body and protective bubble energy that has been drawn into the physical body. The great bubble that surrounded both the energy and physical bodies, and the energy body's bubble, remains and continues to surround and protect the physical body.

8. Begin slowly to trim down the big bubble that continues to surround the physical body, by condensing or shrinking it and drawing it in through the point one and a half inches behind the crown. Add this energy to the pearl that is circulating in the Microcosmic Orbit (fig. 5.15).

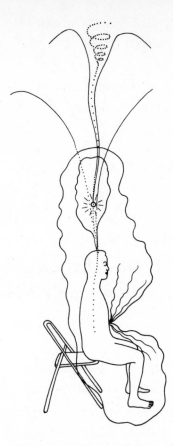

Fig. 5.15. Shrink the energy body's bubble and
draw it into the crown and into the navel.

9. Bring the pearl down the front channel to the navel.
10. You can draw the remaining protective shield in closer and tighter
    to the physical body by drawing this energy in through the navel.
    Feel the energy remaining as the bubble on the outside of the
    physical body as it pulls in tightly to cover the body. You are now
    protected from within and from without by this protective shield.
    As your practice continues, you can continue to form new pearls
    and additional protective shields.
11. Return the pearl to the cauldron. Spiral and condense the energy.
12. Practice Chi Massage.

Formula 6

Forming the Virgin Children and Their Animal Offspring to Connect to the Universal, Cosmic Particle, and Earth Forces

Chapters 6 through 9 describe energy in images. You will use these images to enhance, empower, and protect the organs' energies as you create a more powerful pearl and form a stronger energy body.

The Taoists theorized that, like water, energy is formless. Without giving energy a form, it is difficult to capture its force. Just as water takes on the shape of the jar or pot that contains it, energy can take on the shape of the vessel into which it is placed. Regardless of the vessel's shape, the qualities of the water remain unchanged. Yet, by being contained in the vessel, it becomes easier to use. For example, because you can carry the water, you now can pour the water into a specific place. In doing so you are establishing a connection between the water and that place. Similarly, giving energy a form while retaining its purity helps to establish connections for usage.

Consider religious statues of gods or saints. To help religious devotees form a picture and establish a connection between themselves and a power greater than themselves, they create an image representing and giving form to that power. Once a more understandable picture of that power is formed in the individual's mind, that person can more readily connect with its positive energy. This is the secret power of visualization behind all the world's religions, whether it be the image of Jesus, the Virgin Mother and Holy Child, Buddha, the sacred geometry of Islam, or the numerous gods and goddesses of Hinduism, the Greeks, the Romans, or the ancient Egyptians.

USING IMAGES OF CHILDREN AND ANIMALS TO GIVE FORM TO PURE ENERGY

It is desirable to connect with the positivity and usefulness of energy, and the pictures and images established by the early Taoists become very helpful in making this connection. As a cup or bowl becomes a container to hold water, and as the religious statues, structures, or vessels made from wood, stone, gold, or silver contain a certain power or force, the Taoist images of children and animals also contain energy. Regardless of the shape and material of the container, one is not better than another. All hold the same energy.

The Taoists images of the innocent virgin boy or girl used in association with an emotion are readily acceptable images for most people. This is probably because most people have had experiences dealing with youth or an innocent child and, of course, all of us began our lives as innocent children.

The Taoist animal associations may seem a little unusual, since modern people associate more with domestic animals—dogs, cats, birds. Further, the people of different countries tend to associate themselves with different animals. Below are the animal associations the early Taoists used. You may choose to use different animals or different images, such as a ruby at the heart, an emerald at the liver, and so forth.

Usually people are more observant of the problems of other people or animals than they are of their own problems. When a child, another adult, or an animal gets sick, that being needs care. When others feel depression, fear, or anger, it is a reflection of their inner state. You have to care for them until they heal or overcome such negative emotions. Be aware of the virgin children and animals and keep them in good spirits, and you will be taking care of your internal self.

The Practice of Forming the Virgin Children and their Offspring in the Forms of Animals

Pure Energy from the Kidneys Produces the Blue Virgin Child and the Deer

1. Return your attention to the kidneys and the kidneys' collection point. Sense if the kidneys are cleansed of all negative emotion. This can be clearly indicated by a bright, illuminating blue color, or a strong feeling of calmness and gentleness. Spiral the kidneys' essence to their collection point until the collection point glows with bright light as the feeling of gentleness intensifies.

2. Once the intense, bright color and the sensation of gentleness peak, form the blue light into the image of a virgin boy or girl dressed in the blue color. This image represents the purest form of gentleness. Picture the boy or girl breathing out a blue breath. When enough of the blue breath accumulates, watch it transform into a beautiful deer with antlers. The deer represents a more refined, purer energy of the gentleness virtue. It is the pure essence and consciousness of the kidneys, and can be transformed for the creation of and use by the soul and spirit bodies. Make a

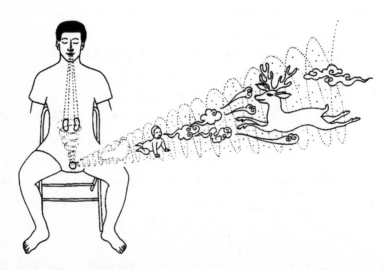

Fig. 6.1. Blue virgin child and deer from the kidneys

strong connection with the blue virgin child and the blue deer, and instantly, at any time, you can restore a sense of calmness and gentleness within yourself (fig. 6.1). The brighter the colors, or the more intense the feeling of virtue, the purer the indication of virtue, and so, good health.

☯ Essence of the Heart Produces the Red Virgin Child and the Pheasant

1. Be aware of the heart and its collection point. Picture the heart's collection point illuminating with bright, red light, and feel a strong sensation of love and joy, the virtues of the heart.
2. At the most intense moment of color and feeling, form the glowing red light into a virgin boy or girl, dressed in the red color. Watch the boy or girl breathe out a red breath, or sense the love, joy, and happiness. Form the breath or the feeling into a red pheasant.
3. Make a strong connection with the red virgin child and the red pheasant, and instantly, at any time, you can restore a sense of love, joy, and happiness within yourself (fig. 6.2).

Fig. 6.2. Red virgin child and pheasant from the heart

❂ Pure Energy from the Liver Produces the Green Virgin Child and the Dragon

1. Concentrate on the liver and its collection point until you can picture the liver's collection point illuminating with a green light or feel an overwhelming sense of kindness.
2. When the green color is at its brightest, or when the feeling of kindness peaks, form the color or feeling into a virgin boy or girl wearing the color green. Watch the boy or girl breathe out a green breath, or feel the intense kindness, and form it into a green dragon.
3. Make a strong connection with the green virgin child and the green dragon, and instantly, at any time, you can restore a sense of kindness within yourself (fig. 6.3).

❂ Lungs' Essence Produces the White Virgin Child and a Tiger

1. Be aware of the lungs and their collection point. Make the collection point luminous with a bright white or metallic color, or feel the powerful virtue of courage.

Fig. 6.3. Green virgin child and dragon from the liver

Fig. 6.4. White virgin child and tiger from the lungs

2. When the vision of color or the sensation of courage is strongest, form it into a virgin boy or girl dressed in the color white. See the virgin boy or girl breathe out a white breath, or feel the sensation of intense courage. Change it into a white tiger.
3. Make a strong connection with the white virgin child and the white tiger, and instantly, at any time, you can restore a sense of courage within yourself (fig. 6.4).

◐ Pure Energy of the Spleen Produces the Yellow Virgin Child and the Phoenix

1. Concentrate on the spleen and its collection point at the front pakua. Observe as the spleen and the front pakua illuminate with a yellow light, or sense the strong feelings of openness and fairness.
2. When the color yellow or the feelings of openness and fairness are very intense, transform the color or feelings into a virgin boy or girl dressed in yellow. The virgin breathes out the yellow breath, or the feeling of openness or fairness increase, and the transformation of breath into a phoenix occurs.

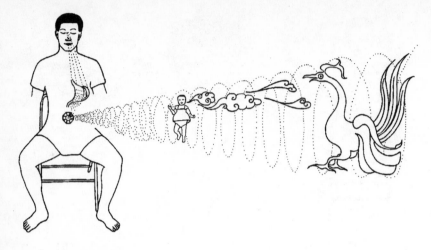

Fig. 6.5. Yellow virgin child and phoenix from the spleen

3. Make a strong connection with the yellow virgin child and the yellow phoenix, and instantly, at any time, you can restore a sense of openness and fairness within yourself (fig. 6.5). The brighter the colors, or the more intense the feelings of virtue, the purer the indication of virtue, and so, good health.

⟳ Use the Virgin Boy or Girl and the Animals to Form Protective Rings inside the Body

1. Beginning at the liver's collection point on the right side, with the virgin child and the green dragon, begin a circle up to the virgin child and red pheasant of the heart's collection point.
2. Then continue the circle around to the virgin child and the white tiger at the lungs' collection point on the left side, and down to the virgin child and the blue deer at the kidneys' collection point. The virgin child and the yellow phoenix are at the front pakua, which is in the middle of the four points of the circle.

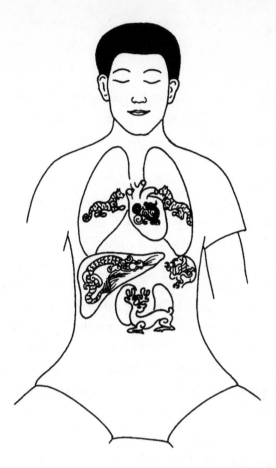

Fig. 6.6. Protective ring of the organs' earth animals

These "power animals" form a protective outer ring around your organs (fig. 6.6). In the inner ring are your virtue energies, crystallized into the different colored virgin boys or girls.

You may choose to create different power animals to protect yourself. While meditating on an organ, you can simply ask, for example: Is there a protective animal that is willing to defend my kidneys/water energy? If no animal appears, you may ask for a "power crystal" or "powerful warrior(s)" to serve you in your spiritual work.

❃ The Pearl Connects with the Universal, Cosmic, and Earth Forces to Supply Energy to the Children and Animals

The pearl will be the center of the gathering of the children and the animals and is enhanced by them. If the pearl dims or disappears, the children and the animals become hard to form.

1. Be aware of the pearl at the cauldron. Feel it shine with the bright light of the silvery or bluish-white color of a pearl.
2. Be aware of the four pakuas, the organs' collection points, the organs, the senses, and their energies.
3. Move the pearl down to the perineum and into the Microcosmic Orbit. As the pearl moves through the Microcosmic, feel the universal, cosmic particle, and earth forces supplied to the pearl. As the pearl moves, the children and the animals can take energy from the pearl as they need it. This energy, in turn, will help to strengthen the organs physically and spiritually.
4. If you wish to continue to the next chapter, there is no need to collect the energy now.

❃ Finish the Meditation

1. To finish, collect the energy, move the pearl into the cauldron, and spiral to condense the energy there.
2. Be aware of the animals and absorb them into the child to which each belongs: the deer to the blue child, the pheasant to the red child, the dragon to the green child, the tiger to the white child, and the phoenix to the yellow child.
3. Be aware of the organs and the child belonging to each one: the blue child to the kidneys, the red child to the heart, the green child to the liver, the white child to the lungs, and the yellow child to the spleen. As you absorb the children into the organs, sense each organ illuminating with a brighter light. This bright light indicates a healthier organ containing a good energy.
4. Practice Chi Massage.

Formula 7

Calling Forth the Earth Force to Empower and Protect

When you have cleared the impure organ energy (negative emotional energy) from the organs and their collection points, they will illuminate with a light that will project outward and attract the earth force. Once you clearly feel the earth force and are able to formulate a very intense picture of the traditional Taoist animals, these images can serve as vessels to make it easier to capture and retain the earth force. This is especially true when you are well practiced. Again, you might have chosen a ring of different magnificent colored flowers or a ring of mighty trees to serve as your earth force guardians.

 ## Calling the Earth Forces

The elemental forces are omnipresent. This means that the five elements of the earth force exist everywhere on Earth. Therefore, you can project the force out in any direction, although in the beginning you will find that it is much easier to project the force to the front. (Note that figures 7.1 through 7.6 demonstrate projecting the force to the front of the body.) When you are well trained, it is possible to project the force to a specific direction associated with the force you want to attract. For example, the force of gentleness can be projected backward, to the north.

The important thing to remember is that whatever kind of force you project out of the body will be the kind you will call forth, regardless of the direction. Just like casting out a baited fishing line to catch a fish, your success will depend on the size of the bait (or your own force) that you cast.

❷ Pure Kidneys' Energy Attracts the Earth Force in the Image of a Big, Blue/Black Turtle

1. Sit facing south.
2. Be aware of the kidneys and their collection point as they illuminate with bright blue light.
3. Sense the virgin child and the deer. When you experience them very intensely, spiral at the collection point. Then exhale through the point. Use the mind and the power of the senses to project an intense wave of gentleness forward to the front, or south, side of the body (fig. 7.1).

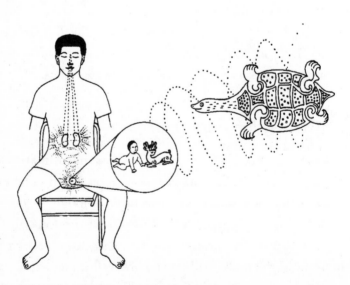

Fig. 7.1. Kidneys, shown projecting to the front, attract the turtle earth force of the north.

4. The greater the force you can project, the greater the amount of watery earth force you will attract.

5. You can sense the force. If you are a more visual type of person, you might see a bright blue force. If you are a more kinesthetic type of person, you might feel the gentleness or calmness of the force.

6. The turtle is the earth force of the north. Once you feel the earth force very intensely, picture the form of a big turtle (also known as the Black Warrior). Put it on your back to protect your back, or north, side.

⊙ Pure Heart's Energy Attracts the Earth Force in the Shape of a Red Pheasant

1. Continue facing south in a seated position.

2. Become conscious of the heart and the heart's collection point.

3. Sense the organs as they illuminate with red light until the red virgin child and the pheasant are clearly perceptible.

4. Spiral the force at the heart and the heart's collection point. Project your force out of the body to its front or south side, to call forth and attract the fiery force of Earth (fig. 7.2).

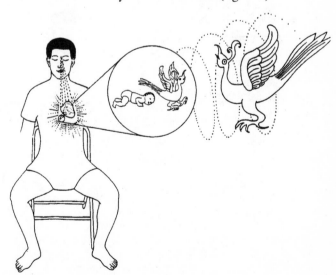

Fig. 7.2. Heart, shown projecting to the front, attracts the
pheasant earth force of the south.

5. The pheasant is the earth force of the south. When you sense the bright red color, or sense love and joyful energy very intensely, form a pheasant to capture the fire force of the Earth. Place the pheasant on your front or south side for protection.

◑ Pure Liver's Energy Attracts the Earth Force in the Image of a Green Dragon

1. Continue to sit facing south. Be aware of the liver and the liver's collection point.
2. Sense the organ's illumination with green light until the green virgin child and the green dragon are clearly perceptible (fig. 7.3).
3. Spiral the force at the liver and the liver's collection point. When you feel the energy very intensely at the collection point, project your force out of the body to the front side, to attract the wood force of the Earth. (If you are able, project the force to the body's east or right side.)

Fig. 7.3. Liver, shown projecting to the front, attracts the dragon earth force of the east.

4. When you sense this green force, or sense kindness very intensely, form a green dragon to retain the wood force of the Earth. Move the dragon to the body's east or right side for protection.

◐ *Pure Lungs' Energy Attracts the Earth Force in the Image of a White Tiger*

1. Continue to sit facing south. Become conscious of the lungs and the lungs' collection point.
2. Sense this organ's illumination with a white light until you clearly perceive the virgin child and the white tiger.
3. Spiral the force at the lungs and the lungs' collection point. When you feel the energy intensify at the collection point, project your force out of the body to the front or south side to attract the metal force of the Earth. (If you are able, project the force out to the body's west or left side.)
4. When you have a strong sense of the white force of the Earth's metal energy, or sense courage strongly, form a white tiger. Move the tiger to the west or left side of the body for protection (fig. 7.4).

Fig. 7.4. Lungs, shown projecting to the front, attract the tiger earth force of the west.

Note: When there is a need for balance in the liver or the lungs, it is possible to call forth the earth animal of each of these two organs to the other's internal animal. For example, the green dragon of the liver, found internally on the right side of the body, can attract the earth tiger force associated with the lungs. You would then place the earth tiger force on the left side of the body to attain balance in the liver. The same is true of the internal white tiger of the lungs and the dragon earth force, with the earth dragon placed on the right side to give balance to the lungs. This method of balance applies only to these two forces.

◎ Pure Spleen's Energy Attracts the Earth Force in the Image of a Yellow Phoenix

1. Continue to sit facing south. Be aware of the spleen and the spleen's collection point.
2. Sense the spleen's illumination with a bright yellow color, or experience a strong sense of fairness and openness.
3. Spiral the force at the spleen and the spleen's collection point. Once you feel an intense energy at the collection point, project your force out of the body to the front or south side to attract the earth force. (If you are able, project the force up through the center of the body through the top of the head.)
4. When you strongly sense the yellow force of the earth's energy, or intensely sense fairness and openness, form a phoenix. Move it to the middle of the top of the head for protection (fig. 7.5).

◎ Form the Earth Force Animals into a Protective Ring and Dome of Fire

1. Reinforce the earth force animals. See them, feel them, or in any way sense the presence of their force and the virgin energy of the earth force.

Fig. 7.5. Spleen, shown projecting to the front,
attracts the phoenix earth force.

2. Form a ring of fire connecting the four animals together: the red
   pheasant, the green dragon, the big, blue/black turtle, and the
   white tiger. The yellow phoenix at the top of the body forms a fiery
   dome that touches and connects the circle (fig. 7.6 on page 118).
3. The dome of fire can protect the physical body by strengthening
   the organs. It can protect the soul body as well. Spiral the dome
   and the pakuas in either direction.
4. As you continue to face south, be aware of the relationship of the
   four pakuas to the four animals: the front pakua to the pheasant,
   the back pakua to the blue/black turtle, the left pakua to the white
   tiger, and the right pakua to the green dragon. Absorb the phoenix force through the crown and down into the cauldron. Absorb
   the forces of the earth animals into the pakuas and then into their
   corresponding organs. Their energy will help to strengthen all the
   organs and glands. (See Table 3 on page 119.)

5. At this point, return to chapter 5 and create a more powerful pearl. Continue to draw energy, including the five earth animal forces, into the front, back, left, and right pakuas and blend it together. Pull their energies into the cauldron to create the greatly refined and radiant pearl that you will use to create a more powerful soul or energy body.

6. Be aware of the cauldron as the pearl becomes enhanced. You can feel the pearl growing bigger and heavier. Move the pearl in the Microcosmic Orbit. Be aware of the universal force from the stars and planets above, the cosmic particle force before you, and the earth force below. Feel the earth force of the animals being absorbed into the pearl (fig. 7.6).

Fig. 7.6. Protective ring and dome of the earth animals

TABLE 3. MORE FIVE ELEMENT ORGAN CORRESPONDENCES

	Wood	Fire	Earth	Metal	Water
Yin organs	Liver	Heart	Spleen	Lungs	Kidneys
Yang organs	Gallbladder	Small intestine	Stomach, pancreas	Large intestine	Bladder
Openings	Eyes	Tongue	Mouth, lips	Nose	Ears
Positive emotions	Kindness	Love, joy	Fairness, openness	Righteousness, courage	Gentleness
Negative emotions	Anger	Hate, impatience	Worry, anxiety	Sadness, depression	Fear, stress
Transform pure organ energy into a virgin child dressed in	Green	Red	Yellow	White	Blue
Transform pure child energy into an animal	Green dragon	Pheasant, red bird	Phoenix, yellow or red	White tiger	Blue deer
Earth force takes the form of	Green dragon	Pheasant, red bird	Phoenix, yellow or red	White tiger	Black tortoise
Directions	East	South	Center	West	North

☢ Create the Energy Body

Using Formula 5, create the energy body, this time with the greatly enhanced pearl. After you have formed the energy body, and if you decide to continue, proceed to chapter 8.

☢ Finish the Meditation

1. If you wish to finish, first absorb the stars' forces as much as possible once more.
2. Condense the energy body into a pearl. Notice that the color of the pearl is intensely bright and its size is larger.
3. Inhale and activate the cranial pump. Feel the pulsation. Feel the lead light extend out from the crown point.

4. Inhale and slowly use the mind and senses to draw in the pearl. Inhale again, and use your mind to guide the pearl to land on the opening of the crown where the lead light emerges. Inhale once more with force to pull the pearl down from the crown through the front channel.

5. Circulate the pearl in the Microcosmic Orbit. As the enhanced pearl moves, it will enhance the organs and glands. Any part of the body that requires its energy will absorb it.

6. Bring the pearl down to the navel and return it to the cauldron. Be aware of the four pakuas and the crown continually absorbing the earth force. Spiral the four pakuas and the pearl, and absorb the earth force into the pearl. Collect the energy in the cauldron.

7. Practice Chi Massage.

8. Now the earth animals force can return to its origin, or it can remain where it is for continued protection. This depends on your proficiency of practice.

Remember that the Universal Tao practice is not solely a visualization process. You must sense the force, not simply picture it in your mind.

Formula 8

Calling Forth the Planets' and Stars' Forces to Empower and Protect

Begin chapter 8 by practicing chapter 1 through 7, ending with "Create the Energy Body" in chapter 7. With time and continued practice, everything will become easier and faster. Once your mind is trained, you will be able to easily control all the four pakuas, the collection points, your internal "weather," the senses, and the emotions. As you spiral the energy, you will perceive all of these as balanced and in harmony, ready to be transformed and condensed into a pearl. All will take place in a few minutes.

In your later practice and when you are well trained, all you will need to do is concentrate on the center of control (the cauldron). Then you will use the mind to turn all the senses inward and condense the pearl. This will require a simple awareness of the four pakuas and all the collection points, organs, and senses.

If the pearl you have formed has a good, shining light, you will be successful in your practice of balancing the energy and transforming the negative emotions. Then, like a factory that is set up properly, all you need do is check the finished product. If the finished product is right, the factory is running smoothly. The pearl is the finished product of your practice.

Create a Fully Developed Pearl; Extend and Maintain the Pearl above the Crown

1. Fully develop the pearl and position it well at the cauldron. Also be aware of the earth animals supplying the force to it. Move the pearl down to the perineum, and then move it through the Microcosmic Orbit until you feel it gain momentum. Be aware of all the sources supplying energy to the pearl. Stop the pearl at the perineum, and feel the full charge of the force at the perineum.

2. Activate the cranial pump, and pull the pearl up to the crown. Totally concentrate your mind and senses on the crown, and feel the pulsation there. Feel the crown breathing, opening and closing. Feel the lead light go out through the opening like a fine string. Check for proper timing, and then inhale once more. Swallow the saliva, and feel the pearl pushing upward at the crown. Feel the crown open.

3. Exhale forcefully toward the crown to shoot the pearl out. The pearl serves as the connection between yourself and heaven. It will enable you to absorb the higher, purer, universal force by bringing it down to your physical body. There it can be processed to a more refined energy you can use.

4. Maintain the pearl about three to six feet (one to two meters) above the crown of the energy body. Use the mind and senses as though they were a wireless control determining the movement of the pearl, moving it up and down, right and left, and in a spiral.

 ## Call Forth the Force of the Planets

Form as many pearls as necessary to complete this exercise.

🌀 Summon the Force of Mercury to the Energy Body

1. Be aware of the physical body, the cauldron, and the kidneys. Sense the blue color or the gentleness force generating from the kidneys.

2. Form a blue or gentleness pearl, and bring this pearl to the perineum.

3. Move it into the Microcosmic Orbit to gain momentum and absorb the forces from all sources. Stop at the perineum and activate the cranial and sacral pumps.

4. Draw the pearl up to the crown, and activate the lead light. Look up with the inner eyes, and sharpen your awareness of the space above you and your energy body, into which you will shoot the pearl.

5. Inhale, swallow the saliva upward, and exhale forcefully up toward the crown. Shoot the pearl as high as you can into the space above you (fig. 8.1).

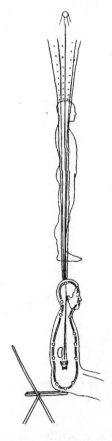

Fig. 8.1. Shoot the pearl high up into the space above you.

6. Exhale. Relax totally, and do the heart's sound (haw-w-w-w-w-w) to attract the universal force and to collect the force as it falls. Feel the universal force fall like blue snow (fig. 8.2).

7. Concentrate your mind and your senses to condense the falling blue snow into the blue planet representing the water force, Mercury. This force will enhance the soul and spirit of the kidneys.

8. Place this force at the back of the energy body (fig. 8.3).

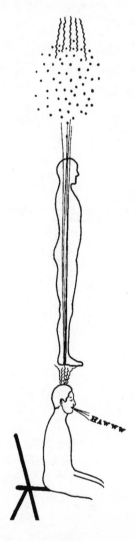

Fig. 8.2. Do the heart's sound—haw-w-w-w-w-w—to attract the universal force. Sense the force falling down as blue snow.

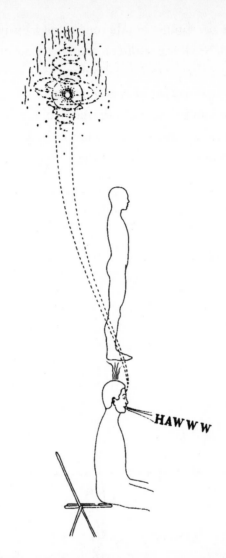

HAW W W

Fig. 8.3. Condense the falling blue snow into the planet
Mercury and place it behind the energy body.

◎ Summon the Force of Mars to the Energy Body

1. Be aware of the physical body, the cauldron, and the heart. Sense
   the red color or force of love, joy, and happiness generating from
   the heart.
2. Form a red pearl or pearl of joy, and bring it to the perineum.

3. Move this pearl into the Microcosmic Orbit to gain momentum and absorb the forces from all sources. Stop at the perineum and activate the cranial and sacral pumps.

4. Draw the pearl up to the crown, and activate the lead light. Look up with the inner eyes, and sharpen your awareness of the space above you, into which you will shoot the pearl.

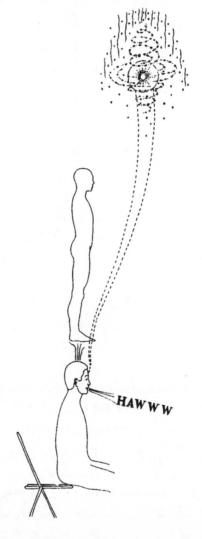

Fig. 8.4. Shoot the pearl up as high as you can into space to connect with the force of Mars. Place Mars's force at the energy body's front.

5. Inhale, swallow the saliva upward, and exhale forcefully up toward the crown. Shoot the red pearl as high as you can into the space above you.

6. Exhale. Relax totally, and do the heart's sound (haw-w-w-w-w-w) to attract the universal force and to collect the force as it falls. Feel the heavenly, universal force fall like red snow.

7. Concentrate your mind and your senses to condense the falling red snow into the red planet representing the fire force, Mars. This force will enhance the soul and spirit of the heart.

8. Place this force at the front of the energy body (fig. 8.4).

◎ Summon the Force of Jupiter to the Energy Body

1. Be aware of the physical body, the cauldron, and the liver. Sense the green color or force of kindness generating from the liver.

2. Form a green or kindness pearl and bring it to the perineum.

3. Move this pearl into the Microcosmic Orbit to gain momentum and absorb the forces from all sources. Stop at the perineum and activate the cranial and sacral pumps.

4. Draw the pearl up to the crown and activate the lead light. Look up with the inner eyes and sharpen your awareness of the space above you, into which you will shoot the pearl.

5. Inhale, swallow the saliva upward, and exhale forcefully up toward the crown. Shoot the green pearl as high as you can into the space above you.

6. Exhale. Relax totally and do the heart's sound (haw-w-w-w-w-w) to help attract the universal force and to collect the force as it falls. Feel the heavenly, universal force fall like green snow.

7. Concentrate your mind and your senses to condense the falling green snow into the green planet representing the wood force, Jupiter. This force will enhance the soul and spirit of the liver.

8. Place this force on the left side of the energy body.

⟳ Summon the Force of Venus to the Energy Body

1. Be aware of the physical body, the cauldron, and the lungs. Sense the white color or force of courage generating from the lungs.
2. Form a white pearl or pearl of courage, and bring it to the perineum.
3. Move this pearl into the Microcosmic Orbit to gain momentum and absorb the forces from all sources. Stop at the perineum and activate the cranial and sacral pumps.
4. Draw the pearl up to the crown and activate the lead light. Look up with the inner eyes and sharpen your awareness of the space above you, into which you will shoot the pearl.
5. Inhale, swallow the saliva upward, and exhale forcefully up toward the crown. Shoot the white pearl as high as you can into the space above you.
6. Exhale. Relax totally and do the heart's sound (haw-w-w-w-w-w) to attract the universal force and to collect the force as it falls. Feel the heavenly, universal force fall like white snow.
7. Concentrate your mind and your senses to condense the falling white snow into the white planet representing the metal force, Venus. This force will enhance the soul and spirit of the lungs.
8. Place this force on the right side of the energy body.

⟳ Summon the Force of Saturn to the Energy Body

1. Be aware of the physical body, the cauldron, and the spleen. Sense the yellow color or force of fairness and openness generating from the spleen.
2. Form a yellow pearl or pearl of fairness and openness, and bring it to the perineum.
3. Move this pearl into the Microcosmic Orbit to gain momentum and absorb the forces from all sources. Stop at the perineum and activate the cranial and sacral pumps.

4. Draw the pearl up to the crown and activate the lead light. Look up with the inner eyes and sharpen your awareness of the space above you, into which you will shoot the pearl.

5. Inhale, swallow the saliva upward, and exhale forcefully up toward the crown. Shoot the yellow pearl as high as you can into the space above you.

6. Exhale. Relax totally and do the heart's sound (haw-w-w-w-w-w) to attract the universal force and to collect the force as it falls. Feel the heavenly, universal force fall down like yellow snow.

7. Concentrate your mind and your senses to condense the falling yellow snow into the yellow planet representing the earth force, Saturn. This force will enhance the soul and spirit of the spleen.

8. Place this force on top of the energy body.

Be Conscious of the Five Planets Surrounding the Energy Body

Sit in awareness of the five planets that you have placed around the energy body to empower and protect it. Sense the glowing light of the planets.

Set the Planets into Orbit around the Energy Body and Absorb Their Forces into It

1. Be aware of the planet Mars moving in its orbit around the Sun. Similarly, start to move Mars into orbit around the energy body.

2. As Mars moves into orbit, it will activate the movement of Venus, Mercury, and Jupiter into orbit. Their orbits form rings of light surrounding and protecting the pearl. You will use these rings of light again in later practice to expand the pearl into an energy body.

⚙ Saturn Provides the Protective Dome over the Crown

Move Saturn into orbit around the top of the crown to form a dome of protective light over the crown.

⚙ Absorb the Planets' Forces into the Energy Body

Focus awareness on the energy body, and use your mind and senses to help the energy body absorb the planets' forces. Notice the pearl changing color or growing larger or heavier.

Energy Body Beams the Planets' and Stars' Forces into the Crown

When the crown of the energy body receives the forces from the planets, it will beam their forces down through the crown of the physical body to the crystal room under its crown. The crystal room, also known as the third vertical room, is situated in the middle of the brain. It is considered the control center for information processing of the pineal gland, pituitary gland, and all other glands of the body. During the Fusion Meditation practice, the crystal room functions as a prism to reflect the rainbow colors down to the organs. You can sense the organs glowing with light (fig. 8.5).

1. Be aware of the purple light of the North Star and the red light of the Big Dipper shining into the crown of the energy body, and then down to the crown of the physical body.
2. Feel the light enter into the crystal room.

The forces of these five planets, the North Star, and the Big Dipper will help to purify and enhance the organs further. The pure essence of the organs that now exists can easily condense at the

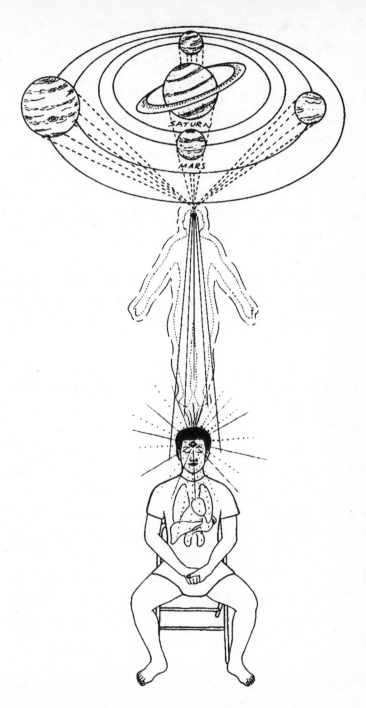

Fig. 8.5. The planets' forces beam down to the crystal room.

crown. The Taoists say that when the five essential forces condense at the crown, they are returning into the Original Force.

 ## Earth Force in the Virgin Children and Animals Interconnects with the Forces of the Planets and Stars

Be aware of the virgin children and the internal animals, of the earth force in the forms of the external animals, and of the forces of the planets and stars. You will find an interconnection, with each force having a relationship to and enhancing another.

- The kidney, the blue child, and the blue deer of gentleness force have a close relationship with the earth force of the blue/black turtle, the northern direction, and the blue force of the planet Mercury.
- The heart, the red child, and the red pheasant of love and happiness have a close relationship with the earth force of the red pheasant, the southern direction, and the red force of the planet Mars.
- The liver, the green child, and the green dragon of kindness have a close relationship with the earth force of the green dragon, the eastern direction, and the green planet, Jupiter.
- The lungs, the white child, and the white tiger of courage have a close relationship with the earth force of the white tiger, the western direction, and the white planet, Venus.
- The spleen, the yellow child, and the yellow phoenix of fairness and openness have a close relationship with the earth force of the yellow phoenix, the center direction, and the yellow planet, Saturn.

Table 4 outlines the completed correspondences of the five elements.

TABLE 4. COMPLETE FIVE ELEMENT ORGAN CORRESPONDENCES

	Wood	Fire	Earth	Metal	Water
Yin organs	Liver	Heart	Spleen	Lungs	Kidneys
Yang organs	Gallbladder	Small intestine	Stomach, pancreas	Large intestine	Bladder
Openings	Eyes	Tongue	Mouth, lips	Nose	Ears
Positive emotions	Kindness	Love, joy	Fairness, openness	Righteousness, courage	Gentleness
Negative emotions	Anger	Hate, impatience	Worry, anxiety	Sadness, depression	Fear, stress
Psychological qualities	Control, decisiveness	Warmth, vitality, excitement	Ability to integrate, stabilize, center, and balance	Strength, substantiality	Ambition, willpower
Transform pure organ energy into virgin child dressed in	Green	Red	Yellow	White	Blue
Transform pure child energy into animal	Green dragon	Pheasant, red bird	Phoenix, yellow or red	White tiger	Blue deer
Earth force takes the form of	Green dragon	Pheasant, red bird	Phoenix, yellow or red	White tiger	Black tortoise
Directions	East	South	Center	West	North
Planets	Jupiter	Mars	Saturn	Venus	Mercury
Universal energy force	Generate	Prosper	Stabilize	Contract	Gather

1. Practice absorbing the forces into the pearl and into the organs and glands of the body.
2. If you wish, continue now to the next chapter.

To stop practicing here, see directions for finishing the exercise on page 134.

Finish the Exercise

1. If you wish to finish your practice at this time, absorb the forces of the planets and stars once more into the energy body.
2. Condense the energy body into a pearl.
3. When you are ready, activate the cranial and sacral pumps to reopen the crown. Feel the crown open, and land the pearl at the crown opening.
4. Inhale, draw the pearl into the crown, and let it start to circulate in the Microcosmic Orbit.
5. Absorb the forces of the planets, stars, and earth. Absorb the earth forces into the four pakuas and the crown. Any remaining energy of the planets, stars, and earth will return to where it came from.
6. Collect the energy in the cauldron.
7. End the exercise with Chi Self Massage.

Formula 9

Transferring Consciousness to the Energy Body in this Life Brings Immortality

The energy body is a chi body that offers no resistance, and so it is very easy to open its Microcosmic Orbit. When you create the energy body and transfer the Microcosmic Orbit from the physical body to the energy body, you are transferring consciousness, as first experienced in chapter 5 of your basic practice and now to be experienced again in your advanced practice.

Each day as you work on this stage of Fusion, you transfer more consciousness to the energy body. At this stage of practice, this energy body is simply a powerful projection of your mind and your physical body. At higher levels of practice, this energy body is crystallized into a permanent spiritual body.

 ## Transfer the Microcosmic Orbit to the Energy Body

Use a Pearl to Open the Microcosmic Orbit

1. Create another pearl in the cauldron and circulate it in the Microcosmic Orbit of the physical body.

2. Inhale, activate the cranial and sacral pumps, activate the lead light, and aim the lead light at the perineum of the energy body. Shoot this pearl through the crown of the physical body and penetrate the perineum of the energy body.

3. Use the senses to move the pearl up to the energy body's sacrum. Stop for a while and feel the sacrum point become established. Then move the pearl up to the Door of Life, T11, C7, base of the skull, crown, third eye, tongue, throat, heart, solar plexus, navel, sexual center, and perineum, completing the Microcosmic Orbit of the energy body. Offering no resistance, the Microcosmic of the energy body is easy to open. Another way to transfer the Microcosmic Orbit is simply to copy the Microcosmic Orbit of the physical body (see fig. 5.13 on page 97).

4. Now begin to move the Microcosmic Orbit in both the energy and physical bodies as one unit by bringing the pearl all the way down the Functional Channel of the physical body. Continue to circulate the Microcosmic Orbit; one cycle should include both bodies (fig. 9.1).

☯ Form a Protective Shield

1. Form another pearl in the physical body, and this time, circulate it in the Microcosmic Orbit of the physical body only until it gains momentum. Once the pearl has gained momentum, and upon its return to the perineum of the physical body, begin to move the pearl up again through the physical body as follows.

2. Inhale, and activate the cranial pump. Contract the perineum, the anus, and the back of the anus. Pull the pearl up to the sacrum, Door of Life, T11, C7, base of the skull, and toward the back of the crown to a point about one and a half inches behind the crown. Hold the pearl at this point.

3. Feel the pulsation at the back of the crown. Exhale, and shoot the pearl out. Use the pearl to form a bubble to cover the entire energy body.

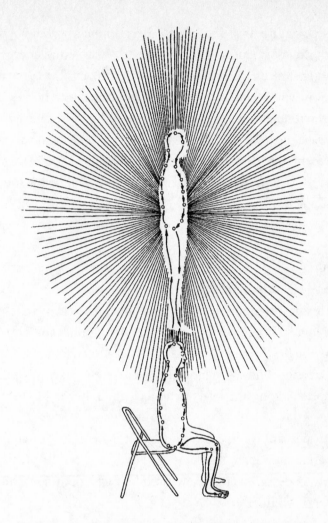

Fig. 9.1. Use the senses and the mind to circulate
both Microcosmic Orbits as one cycle.

Form a Great Bubble Encasing Both Bodies as a Protective Shield

1. Form one more pearl. Circulate this pearl in the Microcosmic Orbit of the physical body to gain momentum. Stop again at the perineum of the physical body.
2. As before, pull the pearl all the way up the Governor Channel of

the physical body to the point one and a half inches behind the crown. Shoot it out from this point to encircle the energy body, bringing it all the way down to cover the physical body as well. You now have formed a great bubble encasing both bodies and the protective shield of the energy body (see fig. 5.14 on page 99).

3. Be aware of the energy body, the physical body, and the bubbles that form the protective shields around both bodies. Also be aware of the energy above the energy body and below the physical body.

⚙ Absorb All Forces into Both Bodies

Up to this level of practice, the energy body is still regarded as a yin body with a negative charge, enabling it to absorb the yang universal force. As your practice advances, the yin body can change into more of a yang body.

The physical body is regarded as a positively charged yang body. This enables the physical body to help channel the yin force from the Earth upward to balance the universal force.

When you are well practiced, all that is necessary to activate all forces is an awareness of them. As an empty vase can be filled, so can the energy body most effectively be filled with the forces, and be a container for them.

1. Be aware of the forces of the virgin children, the internal animals, the external earth animals, and the planets and stars, as they are absorbed into the energy body and the physical body (fig. 9.2).
   • Be aware of the earth force from below emanating a blue force. Sense the force of gentleness and kindness coming up into the feet.
   • Be aware of the forces of the virgin children, the internal animals, and the earth animals, and absorb them into the pakuas and into the cauldron.
   • Be aware of the energy body and the crown.

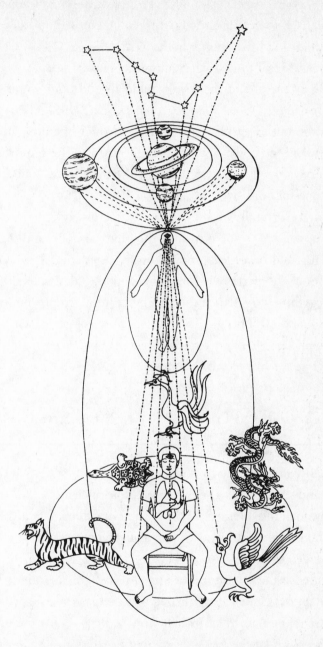

Fig. 9.2. Be aware of all sources of energy.

- Be aware of the five planets and their colors. Absorb the planets' forces into the energy body. Draw the forces into the cauldron of the energy body.
- Be aware of the North Star and its purple light.
- Be aware of the Big Dipper and its red light shining at the crown.

2. Breathe in the purple and red light through the nose and crown of the energy body. Beam this light down to the cauldron of the energy body. These star forces will enhance the soul and spirit essences of both bodies.

3. From the crystalline cauldron of the energy body, beam down the rainbow force to the crown of the physical body, and then down to the cauldron of the physical body.

4. Channel the earth yin force through the physical body to the energy body to balance the energy in it and to prevent excessive heat buildup. The yin force's negative charge drawn from the Earth keeps the energy body's charge in balance.

5. Practice for five to ten minutes.

⟳ Draw in the Energy Body and the Big Protective Bubble

1. When you are ready to finish this practice, first absorb the planets' and stars' forces as much as possible once more. You can leave the remaining energies of the planets and stars. They will return to the Original Force, or will remain to protect you to the extent you need them.

2. Condense the energy body into a pearl still surrounded by the bubble that serves as its protective shield. Notice that the color of the energy of the pearl may now be brighter, or the pearl may have grown larger.

3. Be aware of the big bubble that continues to protect the physical and energy bodies and the energy body's bubble as a great protective shield.

4. Inhale and activate the cranial pump. Feel the pulsation. Feel the lead light extend out from the crown point.

5. Inhale and slowly use the mind and senses to draw in the pearl that is the condensed energy body (see fig. 5.15 on page 101). Inhale and use your mind to guide the pearl to land on the opening of the crown where the lead light emerges. Inhale once more with force to pull the pearl down from the crown through the front channel.

6. Circulate the pearl in the Microcosmic Orbit. As the enhanced pearl moves around the Microcosmic Orbit, it will enhance the organs and glands. Any part of the body that requires its energy will absorb it.

7. Be aware of the energy body's protective bubble remaining above the physical body and within the bigger protective bubble. Be aware of the crown and the point one and a half inches behind the crown. Inhale and draw the energy body's bubble through the crown and the back of the crown into the Microcosmic Orbit, and add this energy to the pearl that is already circulating.

   The energy that now circulates in the Microcosmic Orbit is the combined energy body and protective bubble energy that has been drawn into the physical body. The great bubble that surrounded both the energy and physical bodies and the energy body's bubble remains and continues to surround and protect the physical body.

❂ Protective Shield Remains

1. Begin slowly to trim down the big bubble that continues to surround the physical body, by condensing or shrinking it and drawing it in through the point one and a half inches behind the crown. Add this energy to the pearl that is circulating in the Microcosmic Orbit, and bring this energy down the front channel to the navel.

2. The remaining protective shield can be drawn in closer and tighter to the physical body by drawing this energy in through the navel. Feel the energy remaining as the bubble on the outside of the physical body pulls in tightly to cover the body.

3. You are now protected from within and from without by this protective shield. The protective shield that remains on the outside of the body will be built upon with subsequent layers of bubbles when, as your practice continues, you continue to form new pearls and additional protective shields.

Absorb the Forces into the Pearl or Directly into the Organs of their Origin

1. Be aware of the external earth force animals and of the four pakuas. Absorb the red pheasant through the front pakua, the blue/black turtle through the back, the green dragon through the left pakua, the white tiger through the right, and the phoenix through the crown. Let whatever force remains return to where it originated.

2. Absorb the virgin children and internal animals back into the pearl, or directly to the organs where they belong. The virgin children and animals are the purest forms of the organs' energies. Virtue energy in its purest form can be combined and transformed, and this energy is the consciousness that is transferred to the energy body.

Finish the Practice

1. Condense and draw the pearl that has moved down the front channel into the navel.

2. Bring the pearl to the navel and back to the cauldron. Spiral, collect, and condense the energy at the cauldron. As your practice progresses and the organs' energies become stronger and purer,

the pearl will remain condensed longer. When the pearl finally is released, it will separate and go to the organs and glands that need it as a more refined, more enhanced energy that will heal and strengthen them.

3. Practice Chi Massage.

Summary

The Fusion J Practice

 ### Create a Pearl

1. Smile down to the face and organs; generate a positive emotional state.
2. Smile to the navel and form the front pakua behind the navel.
3. Fuse the senses, organs' energies, and emotions into the front pakua.
4. Form the back pakua, and collect the energy.
5. Spiral the energy or force at the front and back pakuas. Direct the spiral of energy from the two pakuas into the cauldron at the center of the body.
6. Form the right side pakua, and collect the energy.
7. Form the left side pakua, and collect the energy.
8. Spiral the force at the pakuas, direct the energy of the right and left pakuas into the cauldron, and condense the energy to create a pearl there. The pearl will shine with light and glow brighter as more energy continues to fuse from the four pakuas into the cauldron.

Circulate the Pearl in the Microcosmic Orbit

1. Direct the pearl to the perineum by contracting the perineum, the anus, and then the back part of the anus. Move the pearl into the Microcosmic Orbit. At each point—perineum, Door of Life, T11, C7, back of the skull, crown, third eye, throat, heart, solar plexus, and navel—let the pearl illuminate with light. Build up the momentum of the pearl.

2. Bring the pearl back to the perineum, contract the perineum and back part of the anus, and bring the pearl up to the sacrum. Activate the cranial and sacral pumps, and bring the pearl to the crown. Exhale through the crown and project the pearl up approximately six inches (15.23 centimeters) above the head.

3. Use your mind and the senses to move the pearl up and down. Gradually move the pearl higher to approximately twelve inches (30.48 centimeters) above the head.

4. Move the pearl up and down, using the senses to control it.

5. Move the pearl up two feet (60.96 centimeters) above the head.

6. Move it up and down again.

7. Continue to move the pearl up to approximately your body's height above your head.

 ## Form the Energy Body

Focus your attention on forming the pearl into an energy body that looks like you, or into the perfect image you would like to have.

 ## Transfer the Microcosmic Orbit to the Energy Body

1. Circulate the Microcosmic Orbit in the physical body, inhale, and bring it up to the energy body.

2. Move both Microcosmic Orbits separately in the physical and energy bodies.

3. The Microcosmic Orbit can also be run together as one circuit of the energy body and physical body.

 ## Form a Protective Shield and a Larger Protective Bubble around the Physical and Energy Bodies

Form the bubble of the protective shield around the energy body. Then form another, bigger bubble to surround and protect both the energy and physical bodies and the energy body's bubble. The large bubble surrounds you with an aura.

 ## Form the Virgin Children and the Protective Animals

1. Recheck the kidneys and their collection point. Sense the collection point and the kidneys illuminating with a bright, blue light. Feel the virtue energy of gentleness in the kidneys, and form it into a virgin boy or virgin girl. Sense the child breathing out a blue breath that changes into the form of a deer. Place the child and the deer at the kidneys' collection point.

2. Recheck the heart and its collection point. Sense the collection point and the heart illuminating with a bright, red light. Feel the virtue energy of love, joy, and happiness in the heart. Form it into a virgin child, and sense the child breathing out a red breath that changes into the form of a red pheasant. Place both in the heart's collection point.

3. Recheck the liver and its collection point. Sense the collection point and the liver illuminating with a bright, green light. Feel the virtue energy of kindness in the liver. Form it into a virgin child, and sense the child breathing out a green breath that changes into a green dragon. Place both in the liver's collection point at the right side.

4. Recheck the lungs and their collection point. Sense the collec-

tion point and the lungs illuminating with a bright, white light. Feel the virtue energy of courage in the lungs, and form it into a virgin child. Sense the child breathing out a bright, white breath that changes into a white tiger. Place both in the lungs' collection point on the left side.

5. Recheck the spleen and its collection point. Picture the collection point and the spleen illuminating with a bright, yellow light. Feel the virtue energy of fairness and openness in the spleen, and form this energy into a virgin child. Sense the child breathing out a bright, yellow breath that changes into a yellow phoenix. Place both in the front pakua.

6. Form protective rings by connecting the inner animals and virgin children in two circles. Starting from the kidneys, the virgin child and the blue deer make rings of fire to the green virgin child and dragon at the liver's collection point, to the red virgin child and pheasant at the heart's collection point, to the white virgin child and tiger at the lungs' collection point, and back to the blue virgin child and deer at the kidneys' collection point. The yellow virgin child and phoenix remain in the middle at the front pakua.

 ## Call Forth the Earth Force as a Protector and Source of Energy

1. Be aware of and spiral the energy at the kidneys and their collection point. When you sense the force very intensely, project it from the collection point far out to the front of the body to attract the water element force of the Earth. When this force comes to you, and you feel it very intensely, form the image of the big, black or dark blue turtle (the Black Warrior) to capture it. Place the turtle on the back of the body as protection.

2. Be aware of and spiral the energy at the heart and the heart's collection point. When you sense the force intensely, project it from the collection point far out to the front of the body to attract the

fire element force to you. When you feel this force very intensely, form the image of the red pheasant to catch the force. Place the red pheasant on the front of your body as protection.

3. Be aware of and spiral the energy at the liver and the liver's collection point. When you sense the force very intensely, project it from the collection point far out to the front of the body to attract the wood element force. When this force comes to you, and you feel it very intensely, form the image of a green dragon to capture it. Place the dragon on the right side as protection.

4. Be aware of and spiral the energy at the lungs and the lungs' collection point. When you sense the force very intensely, project it from the collection point far out to the front of the body to attract the metal element force. When this force comes to you, and you feel it very intensely, form the image of a white tiger. Place the tiger on the left side to protect that side.

5. Be aware of and spiral the energy at the spleen and the spleen's collection point. When you sense the force very intensely, project it from the collection point far out to the front of the body to attract the earth element force. When this force comes to you, and you feel it very intensely, form the image of a yellow phoenix. Place the phoenix in the middle of the top of the head as protection.

6. Form a ring of fire to link all the animals' forces together. Include the phoenix at the top to form a domelike covering.

Call Forth the Planets' Forces

1. Form a new, bright, blue pearl.
2. Move the blue pearl in the Microcosmic Orbit to gain momentum.
3. Stop at the perineum, activate the cranial pump, and project the pearl up through the crown into the space above you as far as you can.
4. Wait for the water element force of the planet Mercury.

5. Picture the planet Mercury to capture its force. Place it on the back of the energy body to supply the force to the kidneys and to protect the back.

6. Form a new, bright, red pearl. Move the red pearl in the Microcosmic Orbit to gain momentum.

7. Stop at the perineum, activate the cranial pump, and project the pearl up through the crown into the space above you as far as you can. Wait for the fire element force of the planet Mars.

8. Picture the planet Mars to capture its force. Place it on the front of the energy body to supply the force to the heart and to protect the front.

9. Form a new, bright, green pearl. Move the green pearl in the Microcosmic Orbit to gain momentum.

10. Stop at the perineum, activate the cranial pump, and project the pearl up through the crown into the space above you as far as you can.

11. Wait for the wood element force of the planet Jupiter.

12. Picture the planet Jupiter to capture its force. Place it on the right side of the energy body to supply the force to the liver and to protect the right side.

13. Form a new, bright, white pearl. Move the white pearl in the Microcosmic Orbit to gain momentum.

14. Stop at the perineum, activate the cranial pump, and project the pearl up through the crown into the space above you as far as you can.

15. Wait for the metal element force of the planet Venus.

16. Picture the planet Venus to capture its force, and place it on the left side of the energy body to supply the force to the lungs and to protect the left side.

17. Form a new, bright, yellow pearl. Move the yellow pearl in the Microcosmic Orbit to gain momentum.

18. Stop at the perineum, activate the cranial pump, and project the pearl up through the crown into the space above you as far as you can.

19. Wait for the earth element force of the planet Saturn.
20. Picture the planet Saturn to capture the force. Place it in the middle of the top of the head of the energy body to supply the force to the spleen and to protect the center of the body.
21. Be aware of the energy of the stars and the planets and absorb their force into the energy body. Beam it down from the crown of the energy body to the crown of the physical body. Absorb the energy of the Earth into the physical body.

Condense and Collect the Energy

1. Condense the energy body into a pearl.
2. Absorb once more the universal force from above, the earth animals' energies, and the earth energy from the ground under your feet. Inhale and activate the cranial pump. When you feel the crown point of the physical body open, draw the pearl down into the body, and run it in the Microcosmic Orbit.
3. The pearl may feel clearer now, since it has absorbed energy from the heavens and the Earth.
4. Condense the energy body's protective shield (above the physical body and within the great bubble surrounding both) into a pearl.
5. Inhale, activate the cranial pump, and draw in the energy body's protective shield. Add this energy to the pearl that is circulating in the Microcosmic Orbit.
6. The great bubble continues to provide an aura around the outside of the physical body. Condense and slowly begin to draw the big bubble in through the crown. Add it to the pearl and move it down the front channel of the Microcosmic Orbit.
7. Draw it into the navel and bring it to the cauldron. As you do so, the protective shield that continues to surround the physical body is drawn closer and tighter to the body. You are now protected from within and from without by this protective shield. It will be built upon by new pearls and additional layers of protective shields.

Finish the Exercise

1. To finish, collect and condense the energy in the cauldron at the center of the body where the four pakua energies intersect.
2. End with the Chi Massage.

ADVANCED PRACTICE SUMMARY

In advanced practice, the student programs the mind to project the power out, permitting the entire practice to happen at once.

1. Be aware of the cauldron at the center of the body. Spiral the energy using the mind and body. Use the inner eye to direct the energy along the road or pathway of the spiral. To draw the energy inward, spiral very intensely at the cauldron as you also spiral the pakuas. Condense the energy into a pearl. Once the pearl is formed, you can stop spiraling. Be aware of the pearl, the four pakuas, the collection points of the organs, the senses, the emotions, and the balance of all internal energy. If the pearl formed is bright and firm, then all the internal energy is balanced and in good condition. If not, check each area to correct or adjust the imbalance.
2. Be aware of the virgin children, the animals, and the ring formed internally to protect the body.
3. Be aware of the earth force and the earth animals forming the protective ring and the dome.
4. Move the pearl in the Microcosmic Orbit and project it out through the crown to form the energy body.
5. Be aware of or call forth the planets' forces and form an outer protective ring.
6. Connect with the North Star and the Big Dipper and absorb all the forces through the crown and into the energy body. Beam the forces down through the crown and into the physical body.

7. Form the energy body's protective shield and the big bubble protective shield to protect both bodies.

8. Condense the energy body into a pearl and inhale it into the physical body and down to the navel. Absorb the protective shield into the crown and bring its energy down to the navel. Absorb the big bubble into the crown and as you bring its energy down to the navel, feel the big bubble tighten around the physical body in a protective layer. Condense the energies into the cauldron.

9. Practice Chi Massage.

MORE ADVANCED PRACTICE SUMMARY

1. Be aware of the pearl in the cauldron, the four pakuas, the collection points, the organs, the senses, the virgin children, and the animals. Feel centered, at peace, calm, and filled with love, joy, and confidence.

2. Use your mind and the senses to project the pearl out to form the energy body. Move the energy body as far as the lead light projects. Be aware of the planets, the stars' forces, and the protective shields. Absorb all the energy into both the energy and physical bodies.

3. Condense the energy and the protective shields, and absorb this energy into the physical body.

4. Condense the energy in the cauldron.

5. Practice Chi Massage.

MOST ADVANCED PRACTICE SUMMARY

1. Be aware of the cauldron as the center point of the body. Use the mind, eyes, head, and body to spiral. Continue to spiral and simply be aware of the four pakuas and the collection points. Spiral until you feel the pearl form. Be aware of the pearl in the cauldron and move it into and through the Microcosmic

Orbit. Project the pearl out to form the energy body. Move the energy body up as far as the lead light extends.

2. Be aware of the physical body and the force around it. Be aware of the universal force. Absorb these energies into both the energy and physical bodies.
3. When you are ready to finish, simply condense all the energy.
4. Practice Chi Massage.

PRACTICE FUSION DAILY

Students should practice Fusion every day to refine the emotional tone. This will result in the purified energy that is so essential to the higher stages of the Taoist practice. Do not rush the practice. It takes time to grow in your Fusion practice, but eventually you will see good results.

GUIDELINES FOR DAILY PRACTICE

1. The Fusion practice is a daily internal cleanser and can be as routine to you as taking a bath, brushing your teeth, or taking care of your natural body functions. Fusion is a way to balance energy, strengthen mind power, and transform negative emotions—and other unwanted qualities, or garbage energies, that pile up inside the body—into useful life force. The more you practice and transform the negative emotions, the easier it is to handle them. You can assure yourself that your negative emotions will not burst out. You can easily prevent nervousness, depression, or vulnerability. You can readily practice the very important power of forgiveness.
2. Those who feel unstable and are not in touch with their emotions should work longer on the organ energy before proceeding to work with the emotional energy. Fusion is not a process to repress emotions; it is a process to confront and transform them.

3. Once you are in touch with your emotions, you simply need to maintain an awareness of them. Be aware of their energy as they fuse at the cauldron in the middle of, and just behind, the navel. The pearl, formed at this center of the body, represents the energy of your emotions. It feels warm.

4. Constantly be aware of the pearl at the cauldron, at the center of the body. Once the pearl is set and formed properly, the process of controlling the senses and organs continues, and emotional transformation will happen automatically. Becoming aware of the pearl through the Fusion I practice is like being "programmed." Once you are well programmed with awareness of the pearl, you enable all the organs and senses to control and transform your negative emotions in a few minutes.

5. As you practice, you experience peace, centeredness, and balance. After you have finished practicing, the feelings remain and last throughout the day or longer. You can use the pearl as an anchor. Whenever you have free time, or when you are feeling off-centered and restless, become aware of the cauldron and the pearl. You will feel the peace and calmness of being centered, and your self-control will be immediate.

6. Once you are well practiced in transforming the unwanted emotions, and the organs have grown less negative and more positive, it will be easier to identify and be aware of any negative feelings you or others may have. In the beginning you might feel uncomfortable with this awareness, since you are able to feel other people's negativity toward you. However, this negativity may have existed all along, and you were simply not aware of it. It is when too many negative feelings have accumulated that they become exposed or trigger other emotions. This can drain you of your life force and make you feel depressed.

   Now you will be able to identify negative feelings in their very early stages. Therefore, when you feel there is too much negativity toward you, a daily cleansing with Fusion will increase your tolerance. By spending a few minutes to be aware of the pakuas, the cauldron, the pearl, and the transformation of negative emotions, you will very quickly add to your life force.

7. When you feel unsafe, be aware of the earth force, the Earth's protecting animals, and the universal force of the planets and stars. Sense them surrounding you and protecting you, and you will feel secure and stable.

8. The feelings of centeredness and balance are very useful. You can use them to measure the energy of the people you are in touch with to determine whether you can work well together or not. If a person always tilts you off center, and you find it very hard to return to center, you have to find another way to deal with that person. You can choose to have less contact, but if you must deal with the person, it is to your advantage to help them become more centered. Perhaps you can inform them about the very helpful Microcosmic Orbit and Fusion practices.

9. The mind's power and the organs' and senses' power combined with the earth forces and universal forces will give you a very powerful force. You can project this force to accomplish a project properly. You will be doing your work with a sense of good energy, and you will not harm others to benefit yourself.

10. The one true force in the universe is that of virtue. This is the same force as the universal force of the stars and planets. To channel this good force down to you, you need to cultivate the forces of love, kindness, joy, and gentleness. Evil is a destructive force, and it too exists in the universe as a very powerful force. Those people who want to use the force of evil have to channel it through hate, cruelty, and anger, and they will create destruction. However, those who cultivate inner virtue can project the good forces outward toward others. By helping people and comforting them, with no expectations of reward,

the reward will come unexpectedly, with a tremendous growth of inner virtue.

11. Know which force you want to use. Project your choice of force outward, and gradually you will see it manifest in whatever you do. For example, if you want your business to be successful, running smoothly and without harming other people for your own benefit, then picture that business. By gradually manifesting your vision, you will cause it to happen. It will probably involve more of your energy to accomplish this successfully. Therefore, the enhanced strength of the body and its organs from outside forces is very important.

12. When you have a problem in your life, you can place the problem in the energy body, and try to separate yourself in this way from the problem. It will help you to look at the problem from a different perspective.

    Whether the problem be with your work or with your family, if you are weak, sick, or under emotional attack, you will find it very hard to solve problems. Fusion I first will balance, strengthen, and clean the troublesome emotions. Then, once you are able to create an energy body, you can fill the physical body with life force. You will then find yourself stronger and ready to face your problem.

    By placing the problem in the energy body, it will feel like you have stepped out of the ring. From there you can watch other people's activities, and you can see that they make a lot of mistakes, mistakes that you would not see if you were in the same situation. Absorb the earth and universal forces to help.

    By separating yourself from the problem, and looking at yourself, as a spectator, you can see what mistakes you are making. When you merge the two bodies together again, try to solve the problem from inside.

13. Illness also can be placed in the energy body, and you can try to draw more energy from all the sources to help overcome the illness.

14. When you are traveling, the Fusion practice is useful for removing unwanted energy from the rooms of your lodging, or from a conference room on a business trip. When you first arrive, settle down. Sit and practice Fusion I. Form the pearl of kindness and love, and send it out to clear the room. With love and respect you are ensuring that the area is safe and free from disturbances.

15. Follow each step of Fusion I until you feel the results, before proceeding to the next step. Just like growing a tree, the Fusion process cannot be rushed. It takes a year to add just one ring of growth to a tree, and it takes time to grow in your Fusion practice. Simply be aware of the process as it is happening. Practice whenever you have time, but on a regular basis. Eventually you will see results. Once you have mastered Fusion I, you will be ready to advance to the next level of Fusion.

About the Author

Mantak Chia has been studying the Taoist approach to life since childhood. His mastery of this ancient knowledge, enhanced by his study of other disciplines, has resulted in the development of the Universal Tao system, which is now being taught throughout the world.

Mantak Chia was born in Thailand to Chinese parents in 1944. When he was six years old, he learned from Buddhist monks how to sit and "still the mind." While in grammar school he learned traditional Thai boxing, and soon he went on to acquire considerable skill in Aikido, Yoga, and Tai Chi. His studies of the Taoist way of life began in earnest when he was a student in Hong Kong, ultimately leading to his mastery of a wide variety of esoteric disciplines. To better understand the mechanisms behind healing energy, he also studied Western anatomy and medical sciences.

Master Chia has taught his system of healing and energizing practices to tens of thousands of students and has trained more than two thousand instructors and practitioners throughout the world. He has established centers for Taoist study and training in many countries around the globe. In June 1990 he was honored by the International Congress of Chinese Medicine and Qi Gong (Chi Kung), which named him the Qi Gong Master of the Year.

The Universal Tao System and Training Center

THE UNIVERSAL TAO SYSTEM

The ultimate goal of Taoist practice is to transcend physical boundaries through the development of the soul and the spirit within the human. That is also the guiding principle behind the Universal Tao, a practical system of self-development that enables individuals to complete the harmonious evolution of their physical, mental, and spiritual bodies. Through a series of ancient Chinese meditative and internal energy exercises, the practitioner learns to increase physical energy, release tension, improve health, practice self-defense, and gain the ability to heal him- or herself and others. In the process of creating a solid foundation of health and well-being in the physical body, the practitioner also creates the basis for developing his or her spiritual potential by learning to tap into the natural energies of the sun, moon, earth, stars, and other environmental forces.

The Universal Tao practices are derived from ancient techniques rooted in the processes of nature. They have been gathered and integrated into a coherent, accessible system for well-being that works directly with the life force, or chi, that flows through the meridian system of the body.

Master Chia has spent years developing and perfecting techniques for teaching these traditional practices to students around the world through ongoing classes, workshops, private instruction, and healing sessions, as well as books and video and audio products. Further information can be obtained at www.universaltao.com.

THE UNIVERSAL TAO TRAINING CENTER

The Tao Garden Resort and Training Center in northern Thailand is the home of Master Chia and serves as the worldwide headquarters for Universal Tao activities. This integrated wellness, holistic health, and training center is situated on eighty acres surrounded by the beautiful Himalayan foothills near the historic walled city of Chiang Mai. The serene setting includes flower and herb gardens ideal for meditation, open-air pavilions for practicing Chi Kung, and a health and fitness spa.

The center offers classes year-round, as well as summer and winter retreats. It can accommodate two hundred students, and group leasing can be arranged. For information worldwide on courses, books, products, and other resources, see below.

RESOURCES

Universal Healing Tao Center
274 Moo 7, Luang Nua, Doi Saket, Chiang Mai, 50220 Thailand
Tel: (66)(53) 495-596 Fax: (66)(53) 495-852
E-mail: universaltao@universal-tao.com
Web site: www.universal-tao.com

For information on retreats and the health spa, contact:
Tao Garden Health Spa & Resort
E-mail: info@tao-garden.com, taogarden@hotmail.com
Web site: www.tao-garden.com

Good Chi • Good Heart • Good Intention

 Index